GW00995077

ORDNANCE

London Borough of Merton

M00729052

ORDNANCE

EQUIPPING THE BRITISH ARMY FOR THE GREAT WAR

MERTON PUBLIC LIBRARIES	
M00729052	
Askews & Holts	25-Oct-2018
355.8209 WIL	£17.99
MTWB	

PHILIP HAMLYN WILLIAMS

The History Press

Cover Illustrations

Front: (top) A brand new Male Mk IV paid for by the Federal Council
of the Malay States in 1917. (Richard Pullen)
(bottom) Aftermath of the Chilwell explosion. (Perks Archive)
Back and Frontispiece: Chilwell War memorial. (RLC Archive)

First published 2018

The History Press
The Mill, Brimscombe Port
Stroud, Gloucestershire, GL5 2QG
www.thehistorypress.co.uk

© Philip Hamlyn Williams, 2018

The right of Philip Hamlyn Williams to be identified as the Author
of this work has been asserted in accordance with the
Copyright, Designs and Patents Act 1988.

All rights reserved. No part of this book may be reprinted
or reproduced or utilised in any form or by any electronic,
mechanical or other means, now known or hereafter invented,
including photocopying and recording, or in any information
storage or retrieval system, without the permission in writing
from the Publishers.

British Library Cataloguing in Publication Data.
A catalogue record for this book is available from the British Library.

ISBN 978 0 7509 8441 6

Typesetting and origination by The History Press
Printed and bound in Great Britain by TJ International Ltd

CONTENTS

Chilwell War Memorial. (RLC Archive)

INTRODUCTION

Kitchener's 'Contemptible Little Army' that crossed to France in August 1914 was highly professional, but was small and equipped only with what it could carry. Facing it was a force of continental proportions, heavily armed and well supplied. The task of equipping the British Army, which would grow out of all recognition, was truly Herculean.

It was, though, undertaken by ordinary men and women all around the British Isles and beyond. Men fit to fight in the trenches had been called to the colours to do just that; so equipping them was largely the task of those left behind. In time the government recognised the need for skills of engineering and logistics and men with such skills who had survived the onslaught were brought back to their vocation. Women also had a key part to play.

Ordnance is a story of these men and women, and traces the provision of equipment and armaments from raw material through manufacture to the supply routes that put into the hands of our soldiers all the equipment that they needed to win the war.

In writing it, I am indebted to a number of people. Major General Forbes, a senior officer of the Royal Army Ordnance Corps (RAOC), who in 1928 wrote from his first-hand experience the volume of the *History of Ordnance Services* dealing with the Great War; where he didn't have first-hand knowledge, he used the accounts of colleagues who did. George Dewar who, again from first-hand observation, in 1921 wrote of the *Great Munitions Feat*. Then the authors of the histories of the many companies who dedicated their production to the fight. The men who kept diaries and wrote unpublished accounts of their own war, and the National Archives, The Imperial War Museum, the British Library and the Royal Logistics Corps Archive, where their works are kept for posterity. Also, more recent works: Martin Gilbert's *First World War*, R.J.Q. Adams's *Arms and the Wizard*, Kathleen Burk's *Britain, America and the Sinews of War 1914–1918* and Henrietta Heald's *William Armstrong, Magician of the North*. In relation to images, I thank my friend, Richard Pullen, for his generosity in relation to tank images and also for allowing me to draw on his research in *The Landships of Lincoln*. Again, in relation to images, I thank the Royal Logistics Corps archive, the Rolls-Royce archive, the Jaguar Daimler archives, and the University of Glasgow for the use of images from the Beardmore archive.

This volume is very much a prequel to my first book, *War on Wheels*, which was an account of the men and women who mechanised the British Army in the Second World War. In writing *War on Wheels*, I found myself talking about how various characters, including my own father, Bill Williams, and his friend and rival, Dickie Richards, had learnt from their experiences in the First War. I was certain that this was true, but as time went by I needed more and more to try to found out just what those experiences had been, what they had taught them and indeed how.

Ordnance is the result of that search. In writing it, it became clear that it was in itself a story of how the British Army was equipped in the First World War, since that was the core of the experience of those giving their accounts in the book. It was not the heart of it, since, whilst my father never said, I can only believe that the heart for them, as it was for so many, was the sheer horror of it all; I know that my father suffered from nightmares until the day he died. Nevertheless, the task facing them in the summer of 1940 was just how the lessons they had learnt in the equipping of the army in the First World War could help inform the massive task they faced in doing essentially the same in the Second. I chose the date following Dunkirk deliberately, since that was when backs were truly against the wall.

The subject is vast and the sources idiosyncratic, in that it is a matter of serendipity as to what men chose to record and which records survived.

For these reasons alone, this account is very far from comprehensive. It does, though, seek to offer an impression of the issues faced in the differing theatres. In some cases, it homes in on aspects of detail, such as Chilwell, where the records of the National Shell Filling Factory are comparatively extensive, indeed where my maternal grandfather worked as a supervisor. It also follows the particular experiences of certain people, Lieutenant Colonel Omond, for example, who left an extensive account of his experiences as Divisional Ordnance Officer on the Western Front, and SQMS Hawkes, who left diaries of his experience in Gallipoli and France in 1918. There are other accounts and to all their authors I owe a debt of gratitude. I do not hold myself out as a military historian, rather a writer who has tried to tell a story that draws on the writing of others who were closer to the events.

As with *War on Wheels*, I thank in particular Gareth Mears, who kept the archive of the Royal Logistics Corps, for all his help. However, without my parents I would never have found the story of *War on Wheels* and, had I not written that book, I would never have dreamt of writing *Ordnance*. I am so glad I have. Our debt to those men and women is huge.

I thank my publishers, The History Press. Most of all, though, I thank Maggie, my wife of now over forty years, for her encouragement to me in this, my third career.

I

THE BRITISH EXPEDITIONARY FORCE

In September 1939, Dickie Richards, who had command of the huge Ordnance depot at Le Havre, played merry hell when tons of shelving that he had ordered from England failed to arrive.[1] I just wonder whether he was haunted by the description of another huge depot in the same French town a quarter of a century earlier. Richards had served through the four horrific years of the Great War and, like his fellow Ordnance officers, must have been determined to ensure that costly mistakes were not repeated.

Scattered about the gigantic Hangar au Coton and other sheds or wharves were some 20,000 tons of clothing, ammunition and stores of unknown quantities and more arriving daily. The articles were in miscellaneous heaps often buried under piles of forage; wagons had been dismantled for shipment, the bodies had not yet been erected on their wheels, machine guns had not been assembled with their mounts or cartridge belts, guns with their mechanisms, cases of horse shoes with those of nails. The very spaciousness of this immense shed tempted the Base Commandant to use it whenever he was in want of accommodation and, in spite of protests, horses were stabled among the stores and French and Belgian soldiers encamped there. The French were still removing barrels of oil and bales of cotton lying in the hangar when new arrived, and lorries belonging to the Army Service Corps depot, lodged under the same roof, thundered to and fro. Altogether the scene was one of great confusion.[2]

This was the scene, recorded by Forbes, of the Army Ordnance depot at Le Havre in early September 1914, just before its evacuation to escape the German advance.

In human terms, given the alarming number of casualties already suffered, it was the least of the problems facing the British Expeditionary Force (BEF), but, in terms of equipping an army to be able to continue to fight, it was a disaster and one that probably no one had even contemplated.

The British Expeditionary Force, the contemptible little British Army as the Germans called it, had first seen major action at Mons against a vastly larger German force. The result was retreat and a terrible loss of men and guns. Possibly as influential as the numerical superiority of the Germans was the superior power of their artillery. Martin Gilbert

Unloading stores. (RLC Archive)

reports General Gough as saying, 'I turned to the battery commander and said sharply, "For God's sake hit them!" It was Foreman – a splendid officer – but his reply was damning: "I cannot get another yard out of these guns."' Gilbert goes on to explain that the British guns were 13-pounders. Neither their range nor the weight of their shells could match the German 77mm field gun with which they were confronted.[3]

On 12 August, and during the ten days that followed, some 120,000 men made the Channel crossing in remarkable secrecy 'behind a protective shield of battle ships'.[4] The men were accompanied by some thousands of horses but only a few hundred artillery guns, reflecting the view of the General Staff of how the war would be waged. Each of the divisions to which the troops belonged had been fully equipped at the base depot in the UK. They were said to be the best equipped army ever to leave our shores.

George Dewar wrote[5] a remarkable book in 1921 entitled *The Great Munitions Feat* in which he told the story of the production of the army's equipment from a vantage point close to the event, with the benefit of seeing many of the places where the equipment was used and produced, but perhaps without time to reflect. Nevertheless, his observations do shed helpful light. He questions whether the BEF was as well equipped as some suggested.

The equipping of the army had fallen to the men of Army Ordnance Department at Woolwich and the short history of that organisation, written after the war, records the speeding up of the issuing of items and, with overtime and additional men, how this went without a hitch. An appeal had been made for saddles and some 5,000 were received, together with blankets in 'multifarious hues'. A further request for 7,900 sets of officers' saddlery was met with the comment, 'there isn't enough leather in the world for that lot.'[6] The leather was found, and indeed much more.

The supply plan was that formations would go into battle fully equipped and would only be re-equipped when withdrawn for rest. The troops in the front line would receive daily supplies of food, fodder and ammunition, but that was all.

Given this all or nothing plan, each division had a minimal Ordnance Services representation in the field, indeed a tiny one, with one junior officer, known as the Deputy Assistant Director of Ordnance Services (DADOS), one staff sergeant, a horse and a box of stationery.[7] One such DADOS, J.S. Omond, later wrote:

The text book theory that all troops taking to the field were completely equipped proved to be a delusion. The number of blankets per man was two and not one, and the issue of extra blankets was a heavy job for divisional Ordnance Staff to handle when fresh to the country and to the way of work.[8]

ARMY ORDNANCE SERVICES

The role of Army Ordnance Services was quite particular and far reaching. Lieutenant Colonel Tom Leahy, later known affectionately as Uncle Tom, had been one of the first DADOS and had a deep knowledge of ordnance work.

In a lecture Leahy gave in 1916 he encapsulated the ordnance role in a nutshell very much of its time:

> The Army Ordnance Department is, as regards supply of ammunition, guns, equipment, clothing and stores of all kinds, the William Whitely of the Army, and is a good deal more besides, as we shall see later on – for not only is the Department the Agency for the supply of all fighting equipment, but it is also responsible for the care, storage, maintenance, repair and salvage of this equipment.
>
> In addition, therefore, to being the Universal Source of Supply, it is also the Universal Repairing Agency and Universal Salvage Department for the Army, as regards the whole of its fighting stores.[9]

Bill Williams later described the origins of ordnance in a speech for Salute the Soldier week in 1944:

> My Corps, the Royal Army Ordnance Corps, is one of the oldest Corps in the army, as in bye-gone [*sic*] days it was responsible for supplying the Army with bows and arrows and armour for the men at Arms. In fact, I believe in the early stages of our history we planted the yew forests, from which the bows were made.[10]

The job of equipping the army had grown from this beginning, most particularly, with the development of gun powder and cannon. Following the restoration of the Crown in 1660, a Board of Ordnance was formed that was given charge over the castles and forts that defended the kingdom and which would spread through the Empire.

Tom Leahy. (RLC Archive)   Fireplace of fort on Alderney. (Author)

It also had the role of supplying ordnance, that is cannon, powder and shot, to the navy and to supply siege trains to the army when on overseas service.

The early history of Army Ordnance Services[11] was one of checks, balances, excesses and power. No less soldiers than the Dukes of Wellington and Marlborough had held the then prestigious and powerful office of Master General of Ordnance, but it was also held from time to time by powerful civilians. It was not part of the army. Following the Civil War both Parliament and the Crown were keenly aware of its power and the need to keep control of weaponry, and sought to contain it. The warrant setting up the Board of Ordnance set out a detailed structure of checks and balances for the operation of the Office of Ordnance supervised by the board. Forbes[12] suggests that the procedures were followed more in theory than in practice, with shortcomings in both efficiency and effectiveness. It was an age of sinecure offices and the board was no worse than any other institution.

Moving forward two centuries to the experience of the army's supplies in the Crimea, the situation was pretty close to disastrous. There is an apocryphal story of a shipment of boots being sent comprising only those for the left foot. For this reason, and no doubt many others, the office of Master General was abolished and the supply of ordnance was taken into the Army Service Corps (ASC).

The experience of the Boer War again revealed shortcomings and led to the formation of the Esher Committee to review the organisation of the army. One result of the review was the re-instatement of the office of Master General. The Master General's role, though, was manufacture and procurement, with supply coming under the Quartermaster General.

With the growing complexity of the army's needs, a degree of centralisation within the remit of the Quartermaster General was seen as appropriate and an Army Ordnance Department (AOD) was formed at the Woolwich Arsenal comprising officers with appropriate technical skills, particularly with guns and ammunition. To this department were added inspectors of ordnance machinery, who were transferred from the Royal Artillery (RA) and became ordnance mechanical engineers.[13] In parallel with this, the other ranks, who dealt with stores other than food, were formed into an Army Ordnance Corps (AOC); to these men were added the Corps of Armourers and Armament Artificers. Thus a loose organisation that comprised the AOD and AOC had within it the expertise to supply and repair guns and ammunition. It had men skilled in the repair and manufacture of equipment such as wooden wheels; most of the supplies used by fighting soldiers were brought to them on wagons. It had warehousemen who would supply anything from uniforms to horseshoes.[14]

ARMY ORDNANCE SERVICES WITHIN THE BEF

Three distinct elements of ordnance, in addition to those attached to divisions, had crossed to France in early August 1914.

The Director of Ordnance Services, Brigadier Perry, went to Amiens to join the Inspector General Lines of Communication. The Lines of Communication (L of C) were the vital connection between the base and the fighting troops. In supply terms they comprised supply trains, principally for food, fodder and ammunition, which would run to a railhead from which supplies would be taken by lorry or horse to the troops.

The Deputy Director of Ordnance Services, Colonel Mathew, went to Le Cateau to join General Headquarters (GHQ) under the Quartermaster General. This was the planning heart of the force.

Thirdly, there was No. 1 Company Army Ordnance Corps from Aldershot, which would be joined by 2, 3, 4 and 7 companies to establish the base depot at Le Havre under Colonel Egan as Chief Ordnance Officer.

The men comprising the Ordnance Companies were either regular soldiers or reservists who had been called up on the declaration of war. One such wrote to the *AOC Gazette* in August 1914 of his experience:

The writer – a missionary in Egypt – little thought when he left Egypt in June for six months' holiday that he would be called once more to carry arms and learn to dodge parade. Once Austria had declared war upon Serbia, events moved pretty quickly and soon Britain was involved in a struggle in the interests of Righteousness. Much as we all deplore war, certain we can be that Right is with us, and if we are called upon to fight, we can fight as men having clear consciences, knowing that whatever sacrifice we may be called upon to make, it will not be made in vain.

I was conducting service in Clacton when I saw that mobilisation was imminent. The sixpence a day I received for nothing for about 8½ years was a silver link that held me to my duty; and on Monday, August 3rd, I telegraphed to the C.O. [Commanding Officer] Woolwich requesting that my papers be sent to P.O. [Post Office] Clacton in the event of mobilisation. Next morning found me in possession of papers; and early on Wednesday I left for duty at Woolwich. I was amused as I travelled up. Excited territorials stood with fixed bayonets in various stations. Holiday makers were fleeing back in terror from the seaside; and in some stations crowds of infantry reservists dissipated their energy in singing and dancing with sweethearts and sisters! I was made angry when certain minor railway officials refused to allow reservists to travel by their lines because their passes were not exactly in order. Men were sent roundabout ways which in at least one case involved the loss of an hour.

I arrived in Woolwich about midday and saw the Regimental Sergeant-Major, who advised me to go home and get all my papers. This I did, returning at seven p.m. What a crowd we were! Some smart and supercilious, others glad to feel that they would soon be decently clad, and able to get something to eat. Some talked bombastically of the fine jobs they had left; others cursed the day they signed on; some groaned because their time would have expired in a few days; and one unduly loquacious individual informed me that 'he didn't believe in no religion, although he had brothers who were M.A.'s etc., etc.!' There was plenty of exercise of the Englishman's privilege – 'grousing', especially when some were left blanket-less for a time upon corridor floors owing to misappropriations by their comrades. This was, however, soon put right when the C.O. came round on a visit of inspection. I got down pretty early, but could not sleep for the tramp, tramp of restless fellows who tried to work off their excitement by marching to and fro. Patriotic catches, reminiscences, greetings of old fellow 'canteen wallahs', all this was not conducive to sleep.

Next morning an attempt was made to get the Reserves into something like order and uniform. The R.S.M. [Regimental Sergeant Major] wore his voice out, and the men looked like a mob on the barrack square. I volunteered to shout, and for some hours shouted myself hoarse; at last we began to look and feel something like soldiers. It was funny to see the old training reassert itself. Occasionally parties were cheered off – but on the whole one could see we needed to work up some enthusiasm to counteract the pangs of parting with loved ones. The Colonel came and expressed his gratification at the way the men had turned up. It was fine to notice the difference between Ordnance Reserves and those of the fighting units.

Next day we got twisted up in the intricacies of the modern drill. The Adjutant said it was extraordinary to see the smart appearance of the men, considering that they had done no drill for years.

What column dodging went on for the first parades, and how we grumbled when we did parade. Then came the assurance that wives and children would be cared for, and what a change seemed to come over all. With true dogged British resignation, we accepted the inevitable and determined to do our best – and a little over – in the ordeal that lies before us. H.E.E.H.[15]

The variety of backgrounds was huge. Ernest Hutson was a railway clerk and he had to obtain permission from the railway company to volunteer. He remembered being full of enthusiasm, seeking change and actually having no regrets – until it became clear that the war would not be over in six months. He recalled too the shortage of ammunition in the early months.[16]

There was also a need for men with relevant trades. In Bill Williams' archive there is a small book entitled *Handbook for Military Artificers*. This book was aimed at tradesmen whose role would be to work on artillery devices in the field. There are five sections of instructions: Carpenters and Wheelers; Smiths; Painters; Saddlers and Saddletreemakers; and RGA Smiths (those working with steam engines). This goes further to emphasise that at this stage of the war the use of the internal combustion engine was not widespread.

Steam transport. (RLC Archive)

The small book spoke of the England of 1914. Villages would often have a wheelwright and a smith close by.[17] They were both vital parts of the community in the making of carts, wagons and wheels. In military terms the wheel made of wood and iron was fundamental both to transport and to artillery. I was told of a village wheelwright who joined up 'to escape the workshop'. Some former soldiers might be surprised that in less than six months his skill had been identified and he was back making and repairing wheels, though this time for gun carriages and limbers.

Altogether, some thirty officers and 1,360 men of Ordnance Services were deployed in France in August 1914.[18]

Premises were found for the base depot in the form of the recently built Hangar au Coton, which spanned some 9 acres under cover. As already noted, also in this building were Army Service Corps vehicles. A separate repair workshop was set up in neighbouring premises. From the base in Le Havre, a mechanical transport depot was set up at Rouen for the Army Service Corps.

The Ordnance Companies were required to set up an advance depot at Amiens. Forbes[19] questions why such a depot was set up so near to the base. Forbes, who had described the opening scene at Le Havre, had witnessed army manoeuvres in 1913 and had seen at first hand what was going wrong. He pointed out that Ordnance officers simply were not

Wagon wheel. (Author)

GS vehicle. (RLC Archive)

involved in the planning of supplies for the BEF. He had had the opportunity of seeing how the French Army was supplied and to witness in its
methods much that would profit the British. It was only over the years
that slowly and reluctantly that methodology was adopted.

The divisions, though, were the sharp end. Major Jasper Baker was
another DADOS and wrote of his experience that first August and
September. He had seen to the equipping of his division before it left
for France. He tells of the only outstanding stores being bicycles for the
Cyclists Company and field kitchens. On arrival in France the bicycles still had not arrived and so he placed an order in the nearby town
of Valenciennes. He tells how the 'purchase was never effected, as the
bicycles arrived from the base the next day, and, before those ordered
from Valenciennes could be delivered, the town was in the hands of the
Germans'.[20] In the case of the field kitchens he continues:

> The day after the Battle of Mons, I received a waybill by post showing
> that my travelling kitchens had left Le Havre several days before. The post
> arrived at 10 p.m. The railhead for the day was some 40 km away and my
> only means of transport a horse which had already marched since 5 a.m.
> The difficulties of transport here became very apparent. I was informed
> that there would be no room in the supply lorries for Ordnance stores and
> no means of transport for the DADOS to get to the railhead … the next
> day I met Major Cowan from GHQ who informed me that he had seen
> several kitchens offloaded at Valenciennes two days before but that the
> town was now in the hands of the enemy.

The plan of the BEF as regards ammunition was to have the base depot at
Boulogne and then ammunition trains under command of an Ordnance
officer. These would be loaded with a 'standard pack' of ammunition of
all kinds that would then be taken to the railhead for distribution by men,
wagons and horses of the ASC to the fighting troops.

In August 1914 one such train came under the command of Lieutenant
Campbell and during this period of mobile warfare it had an eventful
journey. The train, which became known as 'Campbell's Train', set off
from Amiens. This is how Forbes describes its circuitous route:

> First it went to St Quentin, pushed on to Busigny, and then retired again
> to St Quentin, there to provide ammunition parks with 100 tons of

ammunition. Then came the battle of Mons, after which the train was sent back to Amiens en route for Criel, to the north of Paris. Whilst part of the train however, delayed by a hot axle, was still in Amiens station, fresh orders arrived at midnight of the 26/27th August, giving Noyon as the destination, to which place as much ammunition as possible was to go by road on any lorries that might be available.

By 6am on the 27th the supply of lorries ran dry and Perry, who was on the point of leaving, ordered Campbell to follow with the rest of his ammunition by rail to Noyon. At this time the station was a seething mass of humanity seeking to get away to safety, for there were rumours of Uhlans [Polish light cavalry] having been seen close by; and, on returning after a temporary absence, Campbell found his men had been ordered into a train crowded with refugees.

Campbell was thus faced with contradictory orders but, by careful persuasion, managed to secure an engine for his train to take its valuable load to where it was needed.

A second train was in operation under the command of Lieutenant Cunningham, 'Cunningham's Train', which was to deal with the 'heavier natures' – 6in howitzers and 60-pounders. Dickie Richards, who would go on to the post of Director of Clothing and Stores for D-Day, was later in the First World War to command such an ammunition train.[21]

The original plan was for each division to have a mechanised ammunition park to link the railhead with the points where horse-drawn ammunition columns would take over. These parks were to be under the control of the Lines of Communication. With the constant movement of troops in the early stages of the war, the railhead would change almost daily and with it the lines to the ammunition columns. It soon became clear that the Commander of the Lines of Communication was simply too distant to manage this process and so it fell to the GHQ, and in particular the Deputy Director of Ordnance Services (DDOS) at GHQ. Colonel C.M. Mathew thus had to take control of the whole of the organisation of ammunition supply in the rear of divisions.[22]

The British retreated from Mons towards the French frontier, engaging the enemy again at Le Cateau. In addition to casualties, exhaustion was taking its toll as 'infantry staggered half asleep as they marched'.[23]

The Diary of an Old Contemptible, that remarkable first-hand account by an ordinary solider, describes the retreat day by day. This is but one entry:

A 3-tonner in the mud. (RLC Archive)

28 August: Trek resumed at 3.00am. Every hour we pick up stragglers of various units, all recounting their own tale of whole Regiments being wiped out in the battle … dead horses, sides of beef, boxes of milk, tea, jam, 'bully' and biscuits mark our line of retreat. Dumps could not be formed owing to the hurried retrograde movement.[24]

It is after Le Cateau that we can once again join Major Baker:

On the 28th August we were told that we had come to the end of our retreat and a day of rest was ordered for the morrow. No sooner was this order sent out that indents flowed in, and my staff sergeant and myself spent most of the night and the whole of the next day dealing with these and forwarding them on.

During the 29th, the remnants of the 1st East Surrey Regiment, 3rd Division, which had been badly cut up at Le Cateau, marched in and, having no further use for its regimental transport, handed it over to me enabling me to make good the more important deficiencies in transport in my own division.

The next day I received an urgent indent for picks and shovels to dig trenches. I went into Soissons but found great difficulty in obtaining anything as it was Sunday evening and all the shops shut; but finally, with the assistance of one of the officials of the Marie, I found a French military store with a civilian foreman in charge, who gave me the whole of his stock.[25]

The result of the German advance for the Base Ordnance Depot had been the urgent need to evacuate both Amiens and Boulogne. Amiens proved straight forward and Boulogne was emptied and put on board ship bound for Le Havre. With the army now seriously in retreat, the order came that Le Havre itself was to be evacuated. Chaos ensued. Shipments into Le Havre had arrived with no bills of lading to tell what should have been received. Warehouse systems were not in place to ensure efficient storage and ease of identification. Stores were thus bundled on to ships bound this time for Nantes, with Le Mans as the advance depot.

Forbes offers a description of the scene at Nantes:

> There were cases of service dress, caps, parts of guns and machine guns, bales of horse-rugs and blankets, ammunition, tentage, signalling gear – much in broken packages – mingled with forage, medical, veterinary and other goods just as they had been indiscriminately bundled into the hold; and to sort out this chaos was a lengthy and tedious operation, accompanied by a considerable amount of looting.[26]

Commanders cried out for supplies but, with the chaos and lack of records, none could be located quickly. It was only in time that demands were met from stores taken from Nantes to the advance depot at Le Mans.

Major Baker highlights another major problem from the point of view of the divisions, namely the lack of available transport for Ordnance Services. Quite simply, it was impossible to get up to the front line anything like the amount of materiel being requested.

All the time the Germans were advancing and in particular a second wave swept through Belgium. The French took over the British front line on the Aisne and the British transferred by rail to Flanders, where they arrested the German advance at Ypres.[27]

Another view of the challenges facing Ordnance in this first, mobile, stage of the war comes from Tom Leahy. An article written on Leahy's retirement in 1935 tells that he was DADOS of the 3rd Cavalry Division and in the Royal Logistics Corps (RLC) archives there is a scrap of paper on which he drew a map of the division's advance into Belgium in 1914 together with a rough note of its progress.

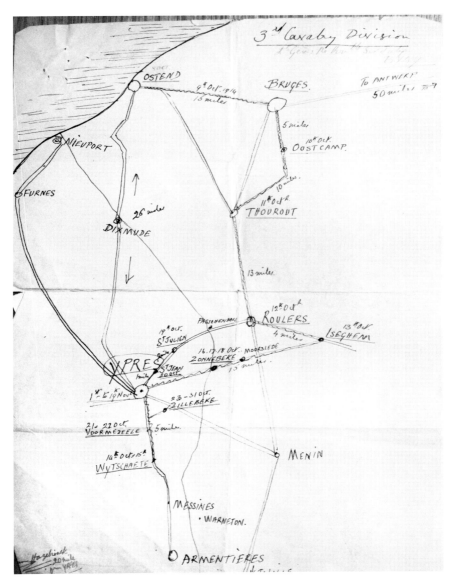

Leahy's map. (RLC Archive)

Private Haylett of the Royal Navy Brigade in an armoured car. (Richard Pullen)

He records that he was appointed on 2 September and one month later was ordered to 'equip the division forthwith'. They embarked from Southampton on 6 October and disembarked at Ostend on 8 October where he immediately requisitioned blankets. He noted that 'wounded [were] arriving'. The diary continues:

> 9 October: rode to Bruges. Met the Belgium Army in retreat also officers and men of British Naval Division.
> 11 October: returned to Ostend to requisition motor tyres.

He goes on to record moving up to Ypres and being caught in heavy fire. On 31 October he writes of a 'lucky' escape for himself but four French officers being killed at our HQ:

> 11 November: very heavy shelling and HQ moved back.

The article on his retirement adds rather more. The force had been hurriedly mobilised under Lieutenant General Sir Julian Byng and was rushed out to Ostend with the object of relieving Antwerp.

THE END OF THE MOBILE WAR AND THE BEGINNING OF THE CHALLENGES OF TRENCH WARFARE

Back in the autumn of 1914, though, the British began to move forward to the line that would be held for the next four years.

The main stores were returned to more appropriate accommodation at Le Havre and this time stored and recorded in an orderly manner.

GHQ was established at St Omer and Headquarters Lines of Communication at Abbeville, where the advanced horse transport depot was also set up providing wagons, harnesses, etc.

Just as there seemed to be a semblance of order, there began to be felt a great scarcity of ammunition and so every hour lost in delivery from Britain became vital. 'Campbell's and Cunningham's trains were despatched to railheads at Aire and Arque, and the rest of the ammunition was concentrated at Boulogne.'[28] The shortage of ammunition was destined to grow into a major problem.

The harsh experience of the first weeks had a number of consequences. Most visibly for Ordnance, General Parsons took over from Brigadier Perry and stayed in post for the remainder of the war. Brigadier Perry would go on to have influential roles in some of the other theatres of war.

Le Havre depot. (RLC Archive)

Mobile workshop. (RLC Archive)

Horse transport. (RLC Archive)

Parsons' great gift was the empowerment of subordinates. For example, as the demands for the repair of guns increased, he brought on to his staff an Ordnance mechanical engineer who could advise on the most appropriate workshop provision. This soon took the form of a number of workshop lorries close to the front.

Yet, the most serious issue that Ordnance officers still faced was how to get supplies to the front. With the onset of the winter it simply was not possible to make troops wait for up to two weeks for replacement boots to cope with the Flanders mud. In the earlier panic of retreat, great-coats and other heavy items had been discarded; these too now needed to be replaced. Divisions were calling for items such as warm clothing, boots, socks, blankets, tents and braziers in immense quantities. What was needed was a systematic way of replenishing equipment and clothing of the troops whilst in the front line.

Forbes identified four related aspects of the problem. The first was transport from the base depot by rail to the railhead. Then there was the shorter but crowded route by horse or lorry from the railhead to the front. Third was the totally inadequate divisional staffing of an officer and staff sergeant. Lastly the task of packing thousands of individual parcels for a rapidly growing army was simply no longer possible.

In relation to transport, the Army Service Corps lorries were jeal-ously guarded for use in carrying food. Trains were filled either with food and fodder or with ammunition with no room for anything else. What Ordnance Services needed was a regular transport service that could take up to the line the supplies that had been indented by the divisional DADOS.

As a result of the Commander in Chief at last recognising the problem, arrangements were made to attach trucks of general ordnance supplies to all food trains headed for the front and for each division's Ordnance officers also to have lorries at his disposal to collect and distribute such supplies.[29]

At the same time, the resource of divisional ordnance services was expanded to become the DADOS with four warrant officers, four clerks, six store-men, a motor car and four 3-ton lorries. Forbes adds a statistic from the summer of 1915 when horse shoes were being expended at the rate of 400,000 per month, with seventeen sizes equat-ing to thirty-four different sorts, each with particular nails. Without this additional staffing at division level, the base depot would have needed to know for each individual unit what horses it had and how heavily they had been worked, which would clearly have been impossible (in that non-digital age). It is interesting that in the Second World War the Army Centre for Mechanisation at Chilwell did maintain a record of which vehicles were in which unit in order to ensure that the correct spare parts were provided.

One of the least easy to understand problems that had contributed to the chaos was the fact that the Army Ordnance Department officers were not informed of what the Master General of Ordnance Department had ordered or was about to deliver.

This problem was overcome with the appointment of Sir John Stevens, a retired Ordnance officer, to the post of Director of Equipment and Stores at the War Office. One of his first acts was to 'send out a list of what stores were due to France from a certain fixed date, and to arrange for a supercargo to accompany each future consignment'.[30] The relationship between Ordnance Services and the Master General would continue to present challenges for many more months.

Forbes recounts one quite particular issue affecting supplies, which would emerge again and again, that he himself witnessed in faraway Marseilles in the latter part of 1914. The Indian Army had sent a number of divisions and these had arrived in the south of France pending transfer to the front in the north. The problem was their totally unsuitable equipment. Their ground sheets were not waterproof and so had to be replaced. None of their rifles were of the same specification as the British and so too had to be replaced together with all necessary ammunition. Indian soldiers provided their own tents, which were simply not up to the demands of northern Europe as it entered the autumn. Much the same went for clothing and boots. All this posed a huge further drain on British ordnance resources.

The particular challenges faced by Ordnance Services in this first stage of the war can perhaps be traced back to the fact that, as Forbes identified back in 1913, it did not have a seat at the planning table and so had to make do with the uninformed decisions of others. Crucially, as has been seen, it had to beg and borrow transport from the Army Service Corps, whose attitude to Ordnance Services may perhaps be summed up in their description of it as 'the bugbear of Ordnance stores'.[31]

This could also lead one to the view that Britain's whole approach to war was somewhat chaotic. The arrangements made for transporting her troops to France, though, would call this into question.

Colette Hooper, and indeed many others, suggests that the foresight of Sir Henry Wilson, the Director of Military Operations at the War Office, should rightly claim credit for the seamless process of moving four divisions to France in a matter of days. Wilson was a Francophile and railway buff. He would spend his holidays on the French–German border and saw at first hand the steps Germany was taking to ensure that it could move large numbers of troops by rail in the event of a conflict. After one such visit, Wilson returned home and, working with London and South Western Railway Company, developed a set of timetables that could transport six divisions to Southampton in the event of war. In the event, six had to be reduced to four and massive additional complications surrounding the actual timing of the declaration of war had to be dealt with. It was a Bank Holiday and so the rail system was filled with pleasure seekers; it was also the time of summer training camps and so thousands of territorials had to be brought home before they could be sent off. The operation was a complete success; some ninety trains arrived at Southampton with only one arriving late.[32]

The effectiveness of transport is further supported by Major W.E. Campbell in his unpublished paper, *The Mobilization of British Army Logistics for the First World War*, where he says:

> During the First World War, it was the collective task of the British Army logistics services to ensure the roots of the flower of victory were fed. The QMG Department succeeded while the MGO Department failed.[33]

At this point transport very much came within the Quartermaster General (QMG) department. As I explain further in Chapter 6, a whole range of vehicles had been commandeered. I explore further the shortcomings of the Master General of Ordnance (MGO) department in Chapter 2.

The experience of the BEF had been traumatic to say the least. The popular view had been that the war would be over by Christmas. Martin Gilbert records the caution with which Britain entered the war. The declaration of war had come on 4 August. The hero of Omdurman, Lord Kitchener, had been appointed Secretary for War and on 6 August had shocked his colleagues on the War Council by saying that the war could be a long one and that two of the army's six divisions should be kept at home to defend the island. The remaining four and one cavalry division could cross to France. Compared to the millions of men being placed in

Daimler lorries and London bus. (Richard Pullen)

the battlefield by the French, Germans and Russians, this was indeed a cautious beginning.

The War Council had then acceded to Kitchener's demand for volunteers and the now famous appeal was made for the first 100,000 men. Gilbert quotes *The Times* as reporting that, 'the crowd of applicants was so large and so persistent that mounted police were necessary to hold them in check'.[34] He cautions, though, against the apocryphal story of cheering in the streets but notes 'an undercurrent of enthusiasm certainly on the part of those putting themselves forward'. My uncle, Bill Williams' brother, told me this on a number of occasions but in a tone that said that he could hardly believe what he was saying.

That this undercurrent of enthusiasm was not universal is apparent from the view of the *Labour Leader* newspaper, 'Workers of Great Britain, down with the war. You have no quarrel with the workers of Europe. Don't make their quarrel yours.'[35] The significance of this reluctance would provide severe challenges to the provision of ordnance over the war years. Indeed, at this early stage government was more concerned that war would reduce demand and so result in increasing unemployment. The concern for Ordnance Services was just how the new volunteer army was to be supplied.

For all the Ordnance Services issues, though, it was the human dimension that had rocked the nation and the young soldiers fighting in its name. Just about half the BEF had been killed or wounded.[36] Some 2km outside Mons there lies the village of St Symphorien, a name that resonates with me as being the saint to whom a much-loved church in Cornwall is dedicated. The Belgian village, though, gained a war cemetery and in that cemetery rest the mortal remains of three particular soldiers, among many others. The first, Private J. Parr, is thought to be the first British soldier to lose his life in the First World War. The other two, George Ellison of the Royal Irish Lancers and George Price of the Canadian Infantry, both died on 11 November 1918 and are believed to be the last Commonwealth combat casualties of the war in Europe.[37] The Alpha and the Omega, perhaps.

It is also impossible to talk of ordnance without recognising its consequences. There was first and most obviously the unimaginable carnage that these powerful guns wrought. Yet, there was more. The first action of the British war witnessed, in addition to the rumoured Angel of Mons, another apparition, as the British official medical history of the war records: 'during 1914 several men were evacuated from France to England having been "broken" by their experiences in the retreat from Mons'. Gilbert goes on to explain that within a month, at the base hospitals in France, Lieutenant Colonel Gordon Holmes, an expert on nervous disorders, 'saw frequent examples of gross hysterical conditions which were associated with trivial bullet and shell wounds'.[38]

This condition became known as shell shock and by the end of the war as many as 80,000 British officers and men had been unable to continue in the trenches as a result. It is certain that equivalent numbers from the other warring nations were similarly affected.

So, in October 1914, the initial scramble was over; the lines were set for the massive armies of Europe to slug it out like prize fighters for the following four years. Ordnance Services in both its branches, that under the QMG and that under the MGO, were about to face challenges that would make anything experienced thus far pale into nothingness.

2

THE HOME BASE AND SUPPLY OF WARLIKE STORES UNDER THE MASTER GENERAL OF ORDNANCE

Woolwich had been the lifeblood of the British Army from the eight-eenth century, since it was where the armaments and ammunition were made and kept. It was also the place from which all of the many of types of army equipment were issued, from saddles and wagons to camp equipment and boots. In October 1914 it was a hive of activity.

Kitchener's New Army of 100,000 volunteers was beginning to take shape and among those who had volunteered was J.S. Omond. He was one of fifteen young officers who reported to the Army Ordnance Corps at Woolwich on a Tuesday in early October 1914. From his unpublished account of his war experience he offers, here, his readers a sense of what Woolwich was like that October:

> On every side there was evidence of war activities. From the great crowds outside the Dockyard and Arsenal gates to the tailor's shops where leather buttons were exchanged at exorbitant prices for brass buttons bearing the regimental arms, work was obviously proceeding at great pressure. Recruits were to be seen in all stages of training and in all manner of garments.

The scenes in Hyde Park have been described by many writers, but the drilling at Woolwich was more interesting to watch. There, gun crews were being taught the rudiments of their work, and drivers were learning to ride and drive at the same time. It seemed more like real training for war than all the marching to and fro that went on all through the first months of the war in the parks of London. The one was necessary for the other, but the atmosphere of the Parade Ground in front of the R.A. [Royal Artillery] Mess at Woolwich suggested a reflection of the battle which was raging less than 200 miles away more forcibly than the pleasant surroundings of Bayswater and Kensington Gardens could possibly do. Anti aircraft precautions were taken in hand at once, and the whole district was plunged into a state of profound darkness which, on a foggy night, made it difficult to avoid tripping over curb-stones when tracing one's way from Mess to quarters.[1]

In the Woolwich Arsenal itself there was the Royal Gun Factory, including the brass and iron foundries, the Royal Carriage Works and the Royal Laboratory where the shells were filled; all this on a site of some 1,200 acres stretching for 3 miles along the banks of the Thames adjoining the Royal Dockyard. The Arsenal supplied both army and navy and, perhaps in the twenty-first century most famously, the Woolwich Arsenal Football Club, which dropped 'Woolwich' from its name and moved to Highbury in 1913.[2]

AOC Red Barracks, Woolwich. (RLC Archive)

The first record of military activity on the site was in 1515 when Henry VIII ordered the building of a vessel *Henri Grace a Dieu*, which was launched at the Woolwich Dockyard. Further down the river was the area known as the Warren, which was fortified as a defence against possible attack by the Dutch in 1667. Three years later the Board of Ordnance bought the neighbouring manor house, Tower Place, and 30 acres as a place to store armaments. It had decided that 'a standing army would be better served by the existence of a place convenient to London where manufacture, proof, inspection and storage of cannon and shot could be grouped together'.[3]

The casting of brass cannon had been carried out at Moorfields. Forbes suggests that the decision to concentrate all casting on Woolwich was a result of an accident that had taken place at Moorfields when recasting guns captured from the French by Marlborough in 1716.[4] He quotes an advertisement in the *London Gazette*:

> Whereas a Brass Foundry is now building at Woolwich for His Majesty's Service, all founders as are desirous to cast brass ordnance are to give their proposals forthwith, upon such terms as are regulated by the Principal Officers of His Majesty's Ordnance, which may be seen at their Office in the Tower.[5]

So, in the first half of the eighteenth century there were on the Woolwich site a foundry for casting guns, a laboratory for making gunpowder and a workshop for gun carriages as well as extensive storage.

The year 1854, the start of the Crimean War, was a crucial one for the Arsenal since it was then that an engineer called John Anderson was appointed to undertake a major programme of modernisation and expansion. He introduced steam power into the foundry and the Royal Carriage Factory. Similar building programmes and modernisation were undertaken at the Royal Small Arms Factory at Enfield, which had been set up after the Napoleonic Wars following bad experience with commercial suppliers, and the Royal Gunpowder Factory at Waltham Abbey.

Much of what Anderson created remained in use until the then-named Royal Ordnance Factory closed in 1967.

Another key appointment was made in 1854, when Frederick Abel took the office of Ordnance Chemist, which had fallen into disuse in 1826. Under Abel the technology of ammunition took major strides with Woolwich as a centre of excellence.

Woolwich 1820. (RLC Archive)

In the latter part of the nineteenth century there were thus essentially three factories: the Royal Gun Factory, the Royal Carriage Department and the Royal Laboratory. In 1891 an electrical generating station was added and over the whole complex further advances in methods were made. In 1899 the Ordnance Factories, as the departments of the Arsenal were known, rose to the challenge of equipping the army for the South African War.

The armament process was in a sense relatively straightforward. The Army General Staff would inform the Master General of Ordnance of its requirements. The Master General would then either request what was needed from Woolwich or request the Director of Army Contracts to obtain quotations from an approved contractor. The quotation would be placed before the Secretary of State and the Army Council and after due discussion a contract would be placed.[6]

In August 1914 the office of the Master General of Ordnance was held by Major General Stanley von Dunlop. He had been appointed following the Esher review of the army when the office was revived following a period of fifty years when it was in abeyance.[7] His staff was relatively small and geared to peacetime requirements. The process for obtaining armaments worked well in peacetime; in the heat of war on an unprecedented scale, the reality was wholly different.

Woolwich was an establishment of some significant size, apart from its physical acreage. On 1 August 1914 the Woolwich Ordnance Factories had some 10,866 employees – all men. In the first week of the war another 1,000 were taken on and by the end of the year, the number had increased to 23,000. The Woolwich site also accommodated Army Ordnance, Navy Ordnance, which was separated in 1891, and inspection departments, the addition of whose numbers would increase the 1 August 1914 figure by nearly 5,000. By the end of November 1917, when output was at its highest, the total number was 96,325 men and women, of whom 57,000 men and 27,000 women worked in the ordnance factories.[8]

Among the employees were engineers and chemists of great ability and inventiveness. It was said that if ever the army wanted anything the first and only response was, 'ask Woolwich'.

If asked what Woolwich made, the response would be guns, of course, but then there were gun carriages, which were arguably more demanding

Red Barracks. Woolwich

Red Barracks, Woolwich. (RLC Archive)

in expertise. There were small arms and small arms ammunition, shells of all calibres for guns and howitzers up to 15in and innumerable accessories.

The shells were for both the army and the navy and Woolwich made them all: cartridge cases, fuses, gaines, primers and detonators. It filled shells from its store of lyddite, cordite and TNT. It then stored shells in dumps spaced at safe intervals over its acres.

It was, though, more than materiel; it was a store of expertise, as would prove invaluable in the war effort to come.

Woolwich became the size of many British cities and the increase in its numbers placed massive demands on the local area. Its workers were housed in huts, hostels and a purpose-built garden city at Well Hall and Eltham. The Woolwich Arsenal Cooperative Society was founded in 1868 by members of the Arsenal workforce and essentially for its benefit.

Women would have a major role at Woolwich, but not until 18 October 1915, after which they 'poured into the filling and small-arms ammunition factories as well as components factories for fuses, cartridges etc'.[9] (I explore the role played by women in chapter 4, page 102)

This then was the core of the British arms industry at the start of the Great War except for key approved contractors and the major shipbuilders. J.D. Scott, writing about the role of Vickers, possibly the biggest of these contractors, noted that in the five years up to 1914 'the great bulk of army supplies had come from the Royal Ordnance Factories: 80 per cent of the guns, and 77 per cent of their ammunition'. With the coming of war all this would change. Scott observed that the 'Royal Ordnance Factories simply didn't have the capacity to supply all that was going to be needed.'[10]

THE APPROVED CONTRACTORS

In addition to Vickers, the other contractors were Armstrong Whitworth, Hadfield, Beardmore, the Coventry Ordnance Factory and the Birmingham Small Arms Company.

Vickers had its origins in the growing metal industries of the eighteenth century. In the mid-nineteenth century, Tom Vickers, a brilliant engineer, came to dominate its business. Scott suggests that engineering was Vickers' passion and really no thought had been given to the possibility of arms manufacture.[11]

There were essentially two main drivers behind the move to armament production. First, armour plating was being revolutionised. The famous iron-clad ships were being replaced by all steel amour, and steel was Vickers' business.

The other driver was the development of the gun and here we have to look elsewhere amongst entrepreneurial engineers.

THE DEVELOPMENT OF THE GUN

William Armstrong was by training a solicitor. His biographer, Henrietta Heald,[12] tells how he followed this rather than his first love of engineering to please his father. Engineering, though, was ever present. Walks on the hills of his native Northumberland had sown seeds of how the power of water might be employed in industry. This led to experiments in hydraulics and eventually the setting up of W.G. Armstrong & Company to manufacture hydraulic cranes.

News of the war in the Crimea brought to public attention the plight of the injured and the need for nursing care, which prompted action by Florence Nightingale. It also highlighted the gross inadequacy of cannons and cannon balls.

Armstrong immediately set to work to develop the better gun that was needed, using the techniques of rifling but also wrought, as opposed to cast, iron. Heald points out that Armstrong was not alone in this; Isambard Kingdom Brunel, who perhaps is best known for the Great Western Railway, was involved, as was Joseph Whitworth, whose name is associated with the standard screw thread and who was also a celebrated engineer of his time. It seems that Armstrong's designs pipped to the post those of Joseph Whitworth and kicked into a play a rivalry that would last decades. The development of the gun was far from simple and demanded many hours of test shots to perfect accuracy, but, more so, a great deal of metallurgy to find the right material to withstand intense pressures as guns became larger and more powerful.

Armstrong was encouraged to develop his ideas, which he did to the satisfaction of the War Office. In a highly patriotic act, Armstrong presented the patents for the gun to the nation and he was appointed to the government position of Engineer to the War Office of Rifled Ordnance. The government then awarded a contract to the Elswick Ordnance

Company, which had been set up by Armstrong but in which Armstrong no longer had any financial interest.[13]

Guns to Armstrong's design were produced at both Elswick and also at Woolwich, where Armstrong was appointed superintendent of the Royal Gun Factory [14] with John Anderson, later general manager, as his assistant.

With the ending of the military crisis, government contracts were cancelled and Elswick had to find its own route to survival. This is it did by supplying arms, in competition with the German Krupp and French Schneider, to other nations.

In 1884 the government encouraged Vickers, Firths and Cammells into ordnance production. Vickers responded by creating an ordnance department to handle gun forgings and it was from this beginning the company's involvement in armaments grew. It was, however, not Tom, but his younger brother, Albert, who would grasp the opportunity. Albert was already the chairman of Maxim, the machine gun manufacturers.

The priority for British defence policy in the late nineteenth century and indeed for a very many decades if not centuries was the navy and this was reflected in the demands placed upon the armaments manufacturers. Vickers acquired Maxim but also shipyards, plants capable of producing shells and, notably, one half of the share capital of Beardmore. Armstrongs acquired its then rival, Whitworth.

William Beardmore & Co. Ltd was one of Scotland's major engineering concerns and, like Vickers, whilst on the War Office lists of suppliers had it hardly produced any armaments for the army before the onset of war. Indeed, its only order had been for two 9.2in guns for coastal defence. Even during the early months of the war orders for guns were not forthcoming and its efforts were initially directed toward shell manufacture.[17]

COVENTRY ORDNANCE WORKS

The Coventry Ordnance Works Limited had its origins in the South African war with armaments produced by H.H. Mulliner and F. Wigley, initially in Birmingham. At the start of the twentieth century the limited company was formed and owned by John Brown & Co. Ltd, Sheffield and Clydebank; Cammell, Laird & Co. Ltd, Sheffield and Birkenhead; and the Fairfield Shipbuilding and Engineering Company of Govern. Its principal factory of some 20 acres was built in 1905 on a 60-acre site in Coventry bordered by the London and North Western and Midland Railway lines and the Coventry canal, a situation that greatly facilitated the transport of raw materials and finished products. From this site it produced guns, gun mountings, shells and fuses. It also had a site at Scotstoun for the 'finishing of naval mountings and appurtenances of war vessels', a filling factory at Cliffe on the Thames and a proving ground on the Wash.[15]

The works were both vast and advanced and more than able to produce very heavy artillery. One of its buildings was thought to be the then largest in the country, being 1,000ft long, 300ft wide and 110ft high to the apex. The boiler house contained three Babcock and Wilcox boilers each capable of evaporating 12,000lb of water per hour at a pressure of 165lb sq in. Adjoining the boiler house was a power plant with two Belliss-Siemens dynamos each capable of developing 500kw at 400 volts. As well as metal working, there was a large carpentry shop for making limbers and wheels; spokes for gun carriages were made of oak naturally seasoned for seven years.

The guns it produced were also huge, one of its lathes was 185ft long. With such large products, many of the albeit very heavy tools were made to be portable so a number could be performing functions on the weapon at the same time. The tools would be slotted into a surface plate 144ft long and 48ft wide.

Before the First World War the Coventry Ordnance Works completely re-equipped the Horse and Field Artillery with 13-pounder and 18-pounder guns.[16] It was most emphatically ready to contribute to the war effort.

RIFLES

The core weapon of the BEF was the rifle and the Birmingham Small Arms and Cycle Company together with the Royal Ordnance Enfield factory were the principal manufacturers. The Birmingham Small Arms Co. (BSA) had been formed in 1861 as an amalgamation of fourteen gunsmiths in the city. In 1881 it added bicycles and parts for them to its products.[18]

Donovan Ward, writing about BSA, explains that, had the war come a year or two later, a much better rifle would have been available. However, in 1914 a choice had to be made between the then current Mark III Short Lee-Enfield, first adopted in 1907 and severely criticised in Parliament, and the German Mauser. Although a factory was in the course of construction at Small Heath for the manufacture of the Mauser, the army chose the existing Lee-Enfield. This proved itself to have been an excellent choice for the conditions that would be found in the trenches.[19] He says that 'its firing qualities in the hands of the Old Contemptibles were such that the Germans were convinced that they had been misled by their Secret Service and that Britain possessed a far greater number of machine guns than had been supposed.'[20]

MACHINE GUNS

Machine guns were quite probably the most contentious weapon for the British. Dewar tells how the scale had been set, largely by Kitchener himself in the interests of economy, for two guns per battalion or a total of twenty-four per division. Adams suggests that it was not 'the broad sweep of strategy or the incisive decisions of tactics which had brought him to the highest place in the army: rather, it was his talent for conducting a campaign of economy, in terms of manpower, supplies and equipment and, consequently, of money'.[21]

J.D. Scott explains that the water-cooled Maxim gun was obsolete in 1914, however those already in service were retained and some more, together with parts, were manufactured in Enfield in the first two years of the war. Dewar writes warmly of the Maxim that in its time it 'easily passed all competitors'.[22] Its prime, though, had been at Omdurman and by 1914 there was ample scope for improvement.

It was Vickers' own machine gun that the army wanted. Scott quotes the *History of the Ministry of Munitions* as saying 'Military authorities were emphatic in their preference for the Vickers' and he goes on to suggest that one of the reasons was that 'every single part was interchangeable'.[23] For the ordnance men in the mobile workshops behind the trenches this was undoubtedly a major advantage.

The Vickers and the Maxim were heavy machine guns requiring a crew, including one to man the belt feed of ammunition, to operate them. The Lewis was much lighter, designed for use by the infantry. Donovan Ward recounts the story of the Lewis gun's development. In 1914 the War Office had already approved the Lewis, which had been designed by Colonel I.M. Lewis, former Secretary of the United States

Ordnance Board. In contrast to the Vickers, it was air cooled and magazine fed. BSA signed a contract with Lewis that made available to him the experimental department at Small Heath. Within eighteen months Lewis had a gun ready to demonstrate at Bisley. It was tested both on an aeroplane and on the ground and proved itself in both areas. Ward records that in August 1914 there were only fifty men employed on the Lewis; by 1916 more than 10,000 were engaged on its production.[24]

George Dewar, surveying this scene in 1921 with the benefit of his own eyewitness experience of the war, described it thus:

> The task confronting the country when called upon to equip not an Expeditionary Force, a mere military adventure within strictly defined limits, but an army of millions of men on the scale of the great conscript Powers, was titanic. Nothing remotely of its nature had ever been before put suddenly on a nation. We were in for an adventure utterly unforeseen, in the course of which we were going to produce 258,400,000 shells; 3,954,000 rifles; 240,000 machine guns; 25,031 field guns and heavy guns and howitzers.[25]

Putting these numbers alongside the orders placed and fulfilled gives a sense of the scale of the change that was being demanded.

GUNS

The Vickers machine gun was manufactured at the company's Erith works in the London Borough of Bexley. Some 1,800 were ordered in the first two months of the war, however in such fits and starts as to reveal a singular lack of any plan held by the War Office. The orders outstripped capacity and only 1,022 were delivered on time. This shortfall in deliveries left the soldier in the trench dreadfully ill-equipped to stand up to his German opposite number, who was using machine guns to devastating effect.

The situation with field guns was much the same. Scott records that on 25 August both Armstrongs and Vickers had each been told that they would be given contracts for seventy-eight 18-pounders. The number ordered increased to 360 by October, all for delivery in August 1915. Taking all orders together, a total of 2,338 18-pounders had been ordered, but in the event only 1,096 were delivered on time.

The War Office had not favoured heavy artillery. The experience of the Boer War had taught the need for manoeuvrability and also the killing power of shrapnel. For this reason, there was little heavy artillery available in 1914 and a preponderance of shrapnel shells, and so there was little available, other than 'a few old six inch howitzers and one 9.2 inch'.[26]

The message had come back from the front that all this had to change quickly and that there was a need for a great many heavy guns in addition to 18-pounders.

Even though they had never made them before, in September Vickers were given contracts for sixteen 9.2in guns (raised to thirty-two in October at Kitchener's insistence). They were also asked to design and manufacture a 6in howitzer. The prototype was ready by February and the War Office immediately ordered four, followed quickly by another twelve.

This experience of design was to set the pattern, with the War Office and, later, the Ministry of Munitions leaning heavily on the armaments manufacturers, with technical input from Woolwich, rather than on the Royal Ordnance Factories as such.[27]

Sir W.G. Armstrong, Whitworth & Co. Ltd, now had factories at Elswick on the Tyne and Openshaw near Manchester. Orders were

Beardmore row of 18-pounders. (Beardmore/University of Glasgow Archives & Special Collections, William Beardmore & Co. Ltd collection GB 0248 UGD 100/1/11/3/page 54)

Beardmore gun barrels in factory. (Beardmore/ University of Glasgow Archives & Special Collections, William Beardmore & Co. Ltd collection GB 0248 UGD 100/1/11/4/page 40)

Beardmore 18-pounder. (Beardmore/University of Glasgow Archives & Special Collections, William Beardmore & Co. Ltd collection GB 0248 UGD 100/1/11/4/page 44)

Beardmore 6in howitzer. (Beardmore/University of Glasgow Archives & Special Collections, William Beardmore & Co. Ltd collection GB 0248 UGD 100/1/11/4/page 42)

Beardmore howitzer in factory. (University of Glasgow Archives & Special Collections, William Beardmore & Co. Ltd collection GB 0248 UGD 100/1/11/3/page 43)

placed in August 1914 for 18-pounder field batteries and 60-pounder heavy batteries. The author of *The Wartime Production of Sir W.G. Armstrong, Whitworth & Co. Ltd* added that 'it is believed that this firm alone made any substantial deliveries of these equipments before the end of that year'.[28]

The experience of Beardmore was a little different. It was the smallest army arms manufacturer, although a substantial engineer. When it received orders for 270 sets of 18-pounder field gun equipment in January 1915, the company set about purchasing new equipment for the manufacture of 18-pounders and 6in howitzers at its plants at Parkhead and Dalmuir. Beardmore had been encouraged by the promise of subsidies and received grants for some three-quarters of the total cost.[29]

Beardmore and the other approved contractors on the War Office list went on to produce many thousands of weapons for the war effort. Nevertheless, the placing of orders in those early months of the war can only really be described as haphazard at best.

AMMUNITION

The number of rifles and indeed larger guns increased broadly in line with the number of recruits. The demands for ammunition turned out to be of a wholly different order. If the demand for guns was linear, that for ammunition was logarithmic. The number of shells fired in the three years of the Boer War was 250,000; in the six months to February 1915, it was more than a million.[30]

In September 1914 rumours began to circulate of shortages of ammunition for the BEF. Lord Kitchener and von Dunlop were all too well aware both of the demands being made and the supplies available. A policy of rationing was thus adopted:

> The daily allowance, for example, of 18-pounder ammunition, was reduced from twenty to ten, and on the Second Army's front after the Battle of Ypres, to two rounds per gun per day. The ration of 4.5 inch howitzer ammunition sank at one time to two rounds per gun per day along the entire front, and the ration of 6 inch howitzers were sometimes as low as six rounds.[31]

One point that had been clear early on was that the shrapnel shell, which was the principal shell used by the British, was nothing like as effective in trench warfare as the high explosive shell used by the Germans and French. Nevertheless, it was essentially a problem of numbers. There was no way in which Woolwich could fill enough shells and so the main contractors came into play.

The process for ordering and producing shells was possibly even more haphazard than that for guns. Scott offers the example of the 18-pounder shrapnel shell. Here orders were placed with Armstrongs but in such haphazard quantities that, as Scott says, 'it is hardly surprising if Armstrong's hardly knew any longer where they were'.[32]

The problem was not only of inefficient ordering; shells were being ordered from the wrong firms. As became abundantly clear later in the war, shell manufacture leant itself to a production line process operated by largely unskilled labour. It was entirely unnecessary to take up the production capacity of skilled engineers. Yet of the 10 million shells on order at the end of 1914, 65 per cent were to come from these engineering companies, with Canada and America (Bethlehem Steel and

American Locomotive Company)[33] making most of the rest and only 812,000 coming from Royal Ordnance Factories.

THE CRISIS

The whole issue of arms production was taken up by the then Chancellor of the Exchequer, David Lloyd George, who first removed the need for Treasury consent to the purchase of arms and ammunition. Adams suggests that his support of the war, compared with his serious reservations about the Boer War, was based on support for Belgium, very much the underdog. Either way, from the very start Lloyd George nailed his colours on the need to win at almost any cost. Adams reports Sir George Riddell noting in his diary on 13 October 1914:

> von Dunlop and the others seemed surprised that they could have any money they required. L.G. said to them: 'What are ten, twenty, or thirty million when the British Empire is at stake? This is artillery war. We must have every gun we can lay our hands upon. We are sadly deficient in guns now. You have never asked me for more money.'[34]

The availability of a sufficient number of rifles was a major concern to the Cabinet Committee on Munitions. At its first meeting on 12 October 1914 Kathleen Burk tells how the War Office representative in the USA was instructed to explore the possibility of obtaining 500,000 rifles from American manufacturers. Some nine days later, when the committee met again, von Dunlop informed them that some 781,000 rifles had already been promised from UK manufacturers for delivery by 1 July 1915. Notwithstanding this an agent was sent to the USA to pursue purchases of 400,000. At the same time the Chancellor, Lloyd George, was also seeking supplies from US manufacturers Remington and Winchester.[35] This duplication of effort accelerated the need for a more coordinated approach to arms production and provision, and I explore this further in Chapter 8.

Perhaps of greater significance, the committee did begin to break through the closed list of arms suppliers with the effect that by 1915 there were some 2,500 firms involved in some aspect of arms production.

Lloyd George's next initiative came on 22 February 1915 when he laid before Cabinet a report on the supply of warlike stores including observations on the enemy's capacity. Here are some of his comments from the document in the National Archive. They follow a rather gruesome comparison of manpower and an acknowledgement that at the start of the war Germany and Austria were far ahead of the Allies in terms of munitions:

> The manufacturing resources at the disposal of the Allies are enormously greater than those which Germany and Austria can command … and, the seas being free to them, can more easily obtain material. I do not believe Great Britain has even yet done anything like what she can do in the matter of increasing her war equipment … All the engineering works of the country ought to be turned to the production of war material. The population ought to be prepared to suffer all sorts of deprivations and even hardships whilst this process is going on.[36]

Adams suggests that this report effectively 'declared war on that inflexible routine-mindedness of Major-General Sir Stanley von Dunlop and the Ordnance Department – and, even more important, on the wartime viability of Liberalism itself'.

There followed a period of months of what might be termed as war by committee. A whole series of committees were set up to look into the problem of the shortage and to come forward with solutions. All the time young men were dying in their thousands.

Notwithstanding this hideous destruction being heaped on the British, von Dunlop supported by Kitchener argued that the present system was the right one with a limited number of clearly expert suppliers, principally Woolwich.

In 1914 the Arsenal had been able to equip the British Expeditionary Force plus providing some very modest reserves. It was, however, entirely ill-equipped to arm an army of continental proportions, even Kitchener's comparatively small volunteer armies. The stories were of men drilling with wooden replica weapons and dressed in blue serge, being the only material then most freely available. The reality on the front was much, much worse.

In von Dunlop's papers in the archive of the Imperial War Museum there is a draft copy of a report that sets out in effect his defence of the approach he adopted. The report is dated 1919 but in it he states that most was written in 1915 when the events would have been fresh in his mind.

Before turning to his particular points, Dewar has his own view on von Dunlop's role. This was a contemporary source but one that seems to take great pains to tell the story. Dewar says this:

> The truth about the organization, the Department of the Master-General of the Ordnance at the War Office in the first ten months of war, is this: it strove honestly to get equipment adequate to the requirements of a great army in the making, but it had nothing like the necessary powers and organization to do so.
>
> It could not cope successfully with the tremendous vital question of labour. As a fact, we did not dispose of that in 1915, or even in 1916.
>
> It had not really the necessary powers in regard to non-armament factories, the ordinary industrial factories and workshops throughout the kingdom which had to be enlisted for State work before we could secure enough shells and guns and other munitions, military and naval.
>
> It was horribly handicapped by the withdrawal of skilled workers by the haphazard and excited voluntary recruiting movement which induced highly skilled men in the engineering and chemical trades to join the fighting forces, and insulted them if they hesitated …
>
> The department of the Master-General of the Ordnance was also handicapped by the fact that, almost on the eve of the outbreak of war, the staff of armament factories had been reduced.
>
> Finally, it was not 'energized' by any fervent munition-making crusade, such as the impetuous one undertaken by Mr Lloyd George in May–June 1915, which seized the attention of the nation.[37]

Lloyd George's 'crusade' is explored in Chapter 4. It is interesting that Dewar's defence and that of von Dunlop are mirrored to some degree in E. Alexander Powell's account of *The Army Behind the Army*, the supply of the American Expeditionary Force in 1917–18. Powell is not a man given to understatement, but when he says that the task undertaken by American Ordnance was probably the largest industrial undertaking ever, we can grasp a little of the context in which von Dunlop was working.

Von Dunlop sets out his points in an orderly manner and begins by addressing the central question of the apparent failure to provide sufficient armaments in the first year of the war. He points to essentially three reasons. Problems with labour and trades union restrictions come first, followed quickly by problems in obtaining the necessary machinery and the buildings in which to house them.[38]

He goes on to observe that even the government could not deal with the labour issues until the passing of the Munitions Act of 1915. He then turns to the accusation about the lack of high-explosive shells and is robust as he claims that he had in fact forced the Expeditionary Force to take HE shells, that he had for some six years been urging the use of howitzers and that he had recognised the need to increase the scale of machine guns. He then refers to the efforts, already noted, that he made to provide more rifles and small arms.[39]

There is little doubt that labour problems were a significant factor in the production shortages in these early months of the war. Scott writes of Vickers that, 'not only was their labour poured off into France, but it was poured off in so haphazard a way that even the remaining labour force was disrupted'. At Vickers' Sheffield works alone 'a thousand young men threw up their work for the trenches'.[40] It wasn't simply the loss of men; it was a distrust on the part of the workers of the management's attempts to replace the men who had gone to war with unskilled labour. Certainly on the Clyde at Beardmore, such attempts met strong resistance. It wasn't, though, only resistance to the introduction of unskilled labour.

A claim was made to the Beardmore management for a 2p increase in engineers' wages, which the employer resisted. David Kirkwood was chairman of the shop stewards' committee and argued that the wage increase was needed, not least because of increases in rents brought about by increasing demand from workers moving to the Clyde from elsewhere. The employers were also desperately short of labour and so brought in 150 men from England. This provoked strikes not only at Beardmore but also at the related Albion Motor Company and other works in the west of Scotland. However, Kirkwood had misjudged the public mood and the strike ended as the strikers were ostracised even by their own union.[41]

The Cabinet responded by appointing ship-owner and industrialist, George Macaulay Booth, to address the labour shortage and setting up a further committee under him to mobilise potential sources of armaments supply.

Despite the very best efforts of Booth and his committee, Lloyd George eventually concluded that a far more radical executive solution was required.

His answer came from an unexpected source. As I discuss in the next chapter, the Dardanelles campaign was a major disaster for the Allies. One result was the resignation of the Admiral of the Fleet, Lord Fisher, who concluded he could no longer work with the First Sea Lord, Winston Churchill. Such was Fisher's public standing and such was the distrust of Churchill among leading Tories that the informal pact between parties that had run since the outbreak of war looked doomed. As a result, a meeting took place between Asquith, Lloyd George and the Tory leader, Bonar Law, at which the plan for a Coalition Government emerged.

Such is the nature of coincidence that the rumour of the shells crisis exploded on the public stage on 14 May with the publication of an article in *The Times* by Lieutenant Colonel Charles Repington on Britain's failure at the Battle of Festubert, in which he wrote, 'the want of an unlimited supply of high explosive was a fatal bar to our success'.[42]

From the point of view of Ordnance, the combination of the change of government and the public outcry stemming from the article had the

Ordnance offices, Woolwich. (RLC Archive)

key effect of moving towards the creation of the Ministry of Munitions under Lloyd George. Another result of the affair was the resignation of Winston Churchill and his decision to go himself to serve on the Western Front, an experience that would inform his later tenure as Minister of Munitions and his role in the development of the tank.

SUPPLY

Whilst all the political manoeuvring was taking place and despite the crisis in production, the day-to-day supply to the army had to continue to the best of the ability of those involved.

The Army Ordnance Department had, in the years running up to 1914, been rather squeezed in around Woolwich 'with its scattered store-houses, some in the Arsenal and some in the Dockyard, intermingled with factory buildings, cramped and badly served by rail'.[43]

The management structure of Woolwich and the Ordnance function more generally may appear to us as odd. The provision and manufacture of armaments and ammunition came under the MGO, as already described. The provision and purchase of all other ordnance stores came under the Quartermaster General who, through the Director of Ordnance and Equipment, also dealt with *all* issues. Both the MGO and QMG sat on the Army Council and were based in the War Office, but as has already been seen, at least initially, they did not really communicate one with the other.

Here, in the lecture he gave, Tom Leahy compares the two sides of the ordnance operation.

The Master General of Ordnance estimates for, provides for, and is responsible for the pattern and manufacture, and inspection after manufacture of the following stores: Guns, Carriages and Mountings, range-finding stores, side arms, Tackles, half wrought stores, carts and wagons, bicycles, ammunition, electric light stores, batteries, cables, telegraph and telephone stores, general engineering stores, (such as survey stores, bridging stores, miners tools, pump, hose and water supply stores), rifles and small arms generally.

Not until fully manufactured does the Quartermaster General or Army Ordnance Department have any responsibility for above. When passed, however, by the Inspection Staff of the MGO as fit for public service, they are handed over to the AOD, who bring them on charge in their ledgers and are hence forward responsible for their care and maintenance.

The QMG estimates for, provides for, and is responsible for the pattern, manufacture and inspection after manufacture of the following stores: Accoutrements (i.e. a soldier's outfit usually not including clothes and weapons), musical instruments, camp equipment, tools etc. for entrenching, metals, timber, harness and saddlery, artificers tools, cordage, signalling stores, oil, paint, chemicals, ironmongery, horse-shoes, waterproof covers and tarpaulins, barrack and hospital stores, textile stores and uniform clothing.[44]

The Army Ordnance Department was responsible for the storage and issue of all items. The role occupied by the Director of Ordnance and Equipment within the ambit of the QMG was explained by Lieutenant Colonel F.K. Puckle, Assistant Quartermaster General British Army, in a talk he gave at Camp Joseph E. Johnston, Jacksonville Florida in January 1918. He had been invited to set out, for the benefit of the then inexperienced US Quartermaster Corps Mobilisation and Training Camp, the British way of provisioning the army.

He explained that the Director of Ordnance and Equipment sits alongside Directors of Supplies and Transport (essentially the Army Service Corps), Quartering, Remounts and Veterinary Services.

In the First World War the Army Service Corps was vast, comprising 12,000 officers and 300,000 men at home and in the field. A sense of the size of the operation may be gleaned from the scale of just one of the reserve depots in England, which held one month's food for a million men, 375,000 horses and 300,000 men in training.[45] Its role was demanding but essentially one of dealing with bulk: food for men and horses. In his unpublished paper, Major Campbell is fulsome in his praise, particularly for the Director, Brigadier General S.S. Long. The story of the ASC is told fully elsewhere.[46]

The role of the AOD was dealing in much smaller quantities of very many more items, each of which had to be delivered to the right place at the right time.

Under the Director of Ordnance and Equipment there was in the UK a home base of Ordnance Services having three strands: clothing, warlike stores and personnel.

PERSONNEL

Looking first at personnel, the question of just who should work in Ordnance Services rather than, for example, in one of Kitchener's volunteer battalions or in the many factories at home producing what the troops required, was not an easy one. Essentially such men needed to be unfit for frontline service because of age or some debility, yet they needed to have the skills demanded in ordnance work. The men required were mechanical engineers, armament artificers and armourers, but also businessmen, chartered accountants, solicitors and shipping agents as well as chemists and physicists. Their numbers increased from 248 officers and 2,273 other ranks in 1914 to 2,434 officers and 39,190 other ranks by the time of the Armistice.

At Woolwich, the Headquarters of the AOD, staffing was modest in comparison with both the production side of Woolwich and the ASC. Just before the outbreak of war the total manpower was 1,450. By October 1915 it had increased to 8,000 men; the figure kept at this level until the end of the war but many of the men were replaced by women.[47]

The impact of the war was that the Ordnance Department at Woolwich had to release 'for duty with the Colours' as many men as possible who were fit for military service. Immediately on declaration of war a fifth of the workforce were called to the Colours. In 1915 a further 621 joined the Colours under the scheme set up by Lord Derby and in 1916 a further sixty-one men were called up under the Military Service Act 1916.[48]

The recruitment of women caused many 'old stagers to shake their heads dubiously'. The women worked to great effect, not only on clerical duties and as packers but also heavy work such as the loading and unloading and stacking of filled ammunition boxes.

The personnel director, Brigadier General Wrigley (QMG 8), had this task of selection as well as pay and conditions not only for soldiers but also for the many civilians who were to be employed in the depots around the country. Forbes makes the point that in spite of labour unrest in many other parts of the civilian war machine, there was none in Ordnance Services.[49]

The job of the Army Ordnance Department included much that was technical. Tom Leahy also talked about its needs in his lecture. He explained that in normal times the Directing Staff of Ordnance Officers would have first served elsewhere in the army and would be selected for transfer to Ordnance having completed an exam in mathematics and mechanics.

Some sixteen such officers each year would undertake a ten-month course at Ordnance College covering subjects including instruction in gunnery material, store accounting, machinery, chemistry, electricity, optics, gun construction, ballistics and general instructions as to the maintenance of guns, all kinds of ammunition and the majority of equipment and stores.

The first course, if passed, was followed by a second year course, following which they would serve for what was in effect a trial or training period of seven years. During this time they would become familiar with the whole job of supplying the army. They would need a thorough command of the contents of what was known as the vocabulary; two thick volumes that contained details of the many different pieces of equipment the army used. They would need to understand the scale of issues.

The scale set out the entitlement of soldiers to the different pieces of equipment. A full set was issued on mobilisation and part of the Ordnance role was to make sure that if more was issued it was truly necessary. The Ordnance officer acted on behalf of the tax payer to ensure that waste was kept to a minimum and there was no profligacy. They would also and importantly be skilled in gun and ammunition inspection.

The massive increase in the size of the department and number of officers placed great strains on this core expertise. Temporary officers would be appointed to roles such as DADOS with nothing remotely like the training and experience to which Leahy refers.

CLOTHING

Clothing (QMG 7) was the strand personally supervised by Sir John Stevens, who had been brought out of retirement to take the post of Director of Equipment and Ordnance Services. Stevens had made his name in the South African war as a man with a great command of detail, but this time he was content to delegate the running of the other two strands to his deputies. Having said this, clothing was no small beer and came under intense strain almost from day one.

As well as Woolwich and the Royal Small Arms Factory at Enfield, the Royal Army Clothing Depot in Pimlico was ranked in the nineteenth century among London's largest employers.[50] The main clothing depot was in Grosvenor Road, not far from Victoria Station, and very quickly it became snowed under, not only with the number of uniforms it had to supply but also with the range of items it had to provide: gum boots and clothing suitable for climates ranging from the desert to the Arctic. Additional accommodation was taken on in London in Battersea, Olympia and White City and elsewhere in Manchester, Leeds, Edinburgh, Glasgow, Dublin and other centres of the textile industry. The Home Commands also had stores for clothing and taken together there were some eighty-five under Sir John's command.

Boot making would become vast and Mr (later Sir Edward) Penton, who ran a well-known firm of leather manufacturers, was taken on and he enlisted essentially the whole of the UK boot-making industry. For those fond of statistics, some 15 million boots were issued to the British Army in France between 1914 and 1918.

In time, with the other changes introduced by Lloyd George in 1915, businessmen, including Lord Rothermere as Director General of Army Clothing, were taken on to deal with the procurement of clothing, but not with its distribution, which would remain with Ordnance Services at Pimlico.

WARLIKE STORES

Notwithstanding the very significant size of the clothing operation, it was QMG 9 Warlike Stores under Brigadier General Seymour that would carry the heaviest burden. These stores came under two main categories. The first, known as QMG stores, were bulky items such as tents, and hospital and camp equipment. The other category, known as MGO stores, were essentially armaments. Early on this category also included ammunition, but this became so vast itself as to demand a War Office department of its own.

Demands for stores would come from the GHQ in France or one of the many other overseas theatres of war and be passed to Woolwich.

In a sense, Woolwich itself was entirely in the wrong place to carry out this key activity, being vulnerable to attack from the air. Astonishingly, in all the war years it was hardly ever bombed. Dewar reports that only once did the Germans hit their target.

Zeppelins first sought Woolwich in February 1915; they did not touch it. They came again several times, without result. At length on

October 13, 1915, six bombs were dropped within the Arsenal. Five were incendiary, and one passed through the roof and upper floor of a machine shop and caused a fire, which was quickly put out, thanks to the pluck and presence of mind of the men in the building. The sixth bomb was a high-explosive one. It burst against a crane in the roof of a machine shop, killing one man and injuring a few others, besides destroying a machine or two. That represented the total damage done to Woolwich during the war by airships and aeroplanes – a humiliating and ridiculous total from a German military point of view.[51]

The Army Ordnance Department already had one historic depot at Weedon in Northamptonshire. There had been barracks and powder magazines at Weedon since 1803. The records show that in 1808 the following announcement appeared in the National Register: 'We learn from undoubted authority that the Government is about to establish an Ordnance Depot at Weedon in Northamptonshire of extra-ordinary magnitude and importance.'[52] Weedon was principally a small arms depot; however, during the First World War it took some of the burden of clothing supply from Pimlico. It had one shed full only of boots.

Didcot was altogether different. The War Office had seen the need to relieve the pressure on Woolwich and also to find a site less vulnerable to attack. The apocryphal story is that a 'senior officer' happened to be standing on Didcot station and saw around him acres of land that looked eminently suitable for a major ordnance depot. Didcot itself was very well placed in terms of communication, being near to the heart of the existing rail network; it was one of the most important railway junctions in the south of England. The site had been identified as long ago as 1889 with the establishment of an army camp nearby at Churn up on the Downs. Whatever the origin of the idea, the records show a purchase in late 1914 by the War Office of 620 acres within the parishes of Didcot, Appleford, Sutton Courtney, Harwell and Milton.

The deeply rural location had the advantages of room for expansion, which most definitely was not the case at Woolwich, and relative safety from enemy attack. The drawback was the lack of a local population to provide the necessary manpower.

Work began on the site in March 1915 with the appointment of contractors, Messrs MacDonald, Gibbs & Co. Sheds were put up to accommodate the 300 soldiers who would be the first to man the depot,

Volunteers from Eton at Didcot. (RLC Archive)

and good progress was made on sheds for storage, roads and railway sidings. On 15 June 1915 the depot opened under the command of Second Lieutenant George Payne of the Royal Garrison Artillery. Payne was soon joined by Chief Ordnance Officer Colonel C. Purchas. Payne described the scene in a letter: 'The stores started to come in from the various factories and soon we turned the previous wheat acres into a seething mass of MUD, MUD, MUD and water. Never did I see such a wet and dismal situation.'[53]

The depot was 'to receive, store and issue stores required to support the British and Commonwealth Armies throughout of the World' but in particular to accommodate the QMG stores that were too bulky for Woolwich, items such as hospital and camp furniture, barrack stores and vehicles. Colonel Purchas clearly reviewed the situation and quickly noted that 'it was becoming impossible with the force of the Army Ordnance Corps here to receive all the supplies coming in from all sources, and to issue them promptly', adding, 'at my wit's end I went to Oxford'.

He visited the commanding officer of the Oxford Volunteer Regiment and soon help began to arrive. Civilians were not permitted and so were encouraged first to join the Volunteer Corps. This they did in great

Didcot swimming pool. (RLC Archive)

numbers, from Oxford colleges but also from the population of Oxford itself, and nearby towns and villages as far as Maidenhead and Banbury. Teachers and pupils came from Eton and Radley, including Prince Henry, later Duke of Gloucester.

The story came to attention of *The Times* and this was part of the article read at the nation's breakfast tables in the autumn of 1915. The headline ran, 'Zeal at Didcot Dons among the workers. Busy Sunday scenes'. It continued:

> The training corps offered to come in a body the following Saturday, and they were joined by a party of Dons and Undergraduates, making a force of between 300 and 400 volunteers …
>
> The work of shunting and unloading went cheerfully forward all that day and the next. Here might be seen a professor painting a bucket, whilst a renowned historian carried plates …
>
> One Sunday, instead of 300 helpers, nearly 3,000 came over from Oxford, Witney, Banbury, Thame, Reading, Maidenhead, Henley, Windsor, Goring and Streatley, Bicester and Chipping Norton. Mr Mason MP, as he stated in the House of Commons on Wednesday, came

over and took command. So well did this amateur army work under the direction of the small regular force that hundreds of trucks were unloaded and the line cleared.[54]

There is some suggestion that the volunteer numbers quoted were an exaggeration. Nonetheless, a great many people did help out. Later in the war the number of soldiers operating at Didcot increased to 1,900. As is clear from a photograph taken in 1917, their welfare was considered important.

Later in the war, Didcot established a magazine area for the storage and issue of small arms ammunition and some 7 million rounds were sent out to France and beyond.

In early 1915, the storage of ammunition was the least of the worries of Army Ordnance. As soon as a shell was produced it was dispatched to France for immediate use.

Didcot certainly eased some of the pressure on the AOD at Woolwich, but, in the summer of 1915, the crisis of armaments and ammunition most certainly had not gone away.

3

GALLIPOLI, SALONIKA AND EAST AFRICA

SQMS Comley Hawkes. (RLC Archive)

Staff Quarter Master Sergeant Comley Hawkes A.O.C., then of the 2nd Hampshire Regiment, wrote a diary of his experience in Gallipoli. I suspect that he wasn't a great sailor since the entries for the first three days of the outward voyage describe him as feeling ill. The ship left England on 21 March 1915 and arrived in Alexandria on 1 April. En route he writes of the 'ripping time' they had in Malta where, on leaving, they were cheered by the crew of the French battleship *Paris*. On 22 April they left Alex on a different ship and came into Lemnos two days later. It reminded him of Lulworth.

'As one looks round the harbour and notes the stillness and the green hills with the little windmills on, it seems impossible that war is so near.' He counted some fifty troopships and battleships in the harbour.[1]

January 1915 had brought a sense of stalemate to the Allies, but, as Martin Gilbert recounts, this in no way diminished the territorial ambitions of the politicians. It was during the meeting of the British Cabinet on 7 January that Secretary of State for War, Lord Kitchener, expressed the view that, in the search for new allies and new war zones, 'the Dardanelles appear to be the most suitable objective, as an attack could be made in co-operation with the fleet'.

It seems that an attack in this geographical region could have a wide range of advantages. It would bring neighbouring countries Greece, Bulgaria, Romania and Italy off their fence of neutrality and into the Allied camp. Turkey would capitulate quickly and some thought it might even change sides. Turkish territory could be divided up and apportioned between the Allied powers, giving something to everyone. The War Council's Secretary, Colonel Hankey, thought success in the Dardanelles 'would give us the Danube as a line of communications for an army penetrating into the heart of Austria, and bring our sea power in the middle of Europe'.[2]

In 1914 and into 1915 British military might depended upon the navy, which still ruled the waves. The Dardanelles campaign was thus conceived by the Secretary of State for War as a naval enterprise. British ships would pound the coastal defences, essentially crushing Ottoman resistance. It was only then that the army would go ashore to secure the territory.

The operation began on 19 February when the fleet attacked the forts at Sedd-ul-Bahr and Kum Kale. Six days later, the bombardment was repeated and the forts were destroyed, Gilbert adding with the unintended advantage to the defenders of providing cover in subsequent action for machine gunners and artillery. The naval attack on the Dardanelles began on 18 March and was, Gilbert suggests, very nearly successful. The Russians joined in the attack but gales made subsequent minesweeping impossible. The chance of swift victory had gone.

The naval bombardments were to be followed up by a sea-borne invasion. Delay meant that the Turks had time to prepare. Germany provided expertise, both Bulgaria and Romania allowed the delivery of vital armaments and labour battalions drawn of a number of nationalities built trenches, laid barbed wire on beaches and generally prepared for defence.

The plan for ordnance supplies was to set up a supply base on the island of Lemnos and two Ordnance officers travelled out in February 1915 to assess the possibilities. They found that the island had no pier to land supplies from large ships and so an alternative was sought.

Alexandria was the main commercial port of Egypt where there was already a British Army presence in its capacity as protectorate. Alexandria also offered ample space, local sources of supply and a good port fed through the British-controlled Mediterranean. Local supplies came into their own later in the war, and the existence of railway companies, for example, which could divert their production to gun parts greatly relieved the burden on UK manufacturers. It may actually be more true to say that without local manufacturing vital supplies simply would not have been available.[3] Alexandria was the perfect Levantine base for the Allies.

The Alexandria base began life in early 1915 with a handful of men and few stores drawn from the existing Ordnance presence in both Alexandria and Cairo. In time Colonel Jackson, who had great experience in provisioning from the South African war, was appointed Director of Ordnance Services (DOS). Provisioning was all about estimating future requirements and would become essential as Alexandria in many ways took over from Woolwich and Pimlico in supplying not only Gallipoli but also Salonika and later Palestine, Mesopotamia and East Africa

Colonel Bainbridge, a very experienced former artillery officer, was appointed DDOS to GHQ of the Mediterranean Expeditionary Force in March 1915.[4] He would deal with matters in Gallipoli, with Colonel Jackson feeding supplies through Alexandria. The revised supply plan was to ship the main supplies from the UK to Alexandria and then to send them on to Lemnos aboard smaller shipping better suited to the island's facilities.

The process of getting supplies from Lemnos to the invading troops was to be by means of two ships. The model was in a sense simple: a floating ordnance warehouse close enough to the troops to replenish supplies at short notice, but far enough away to escape enemy attack. Stores would be set out on shelving in every available space, but most particularly the cargo holds.

The first was a 3,000-ton steamship named *Umsinga* and was fitted out to its new use in Tilbury. Lieutenant Colonel McCheane was appointed Chief Ordnance Officer with a staff of 150 AOC men. When it arrived in Lemnos, a workshop was added on the main deck. The plan for the attack, though, had changed and there were to be two beach landings rather than one. The 29th Division, comprising mainly former British regular soldiers, would attack Helles, and troops from Australia and New Zealand, who were already in Egypt to defend it from Turkish raids, would attack Anzac. A further ship was thus required and the *Anglo-Indian* was fitted out and a part of the stores on board the *Umsinga* transferred. The COO of the *Anglo-Indian* was Major Basil Hill, who would go on to lead the RAOC in the run-up to the Second World War.

Notwithstanding the time that the Turks and their allies had had to prepare defences, the planners at the War Office still believed that the landings would take place without much opposition and that, once landed, territory would be quickly secured and land-based depots could be set up.

A great flotilla of men-of-war and transports gathered in Mudros Bay in Lemnos in the first weeks of April. The fleet sailed for Gallipoli in the early hours of 25 April and by daybreak landings were taking place with the 29th Division at Helles and the Australians and New Zealanders at Anzac. The attacks seemed initially to have taken the Turks by surprise and beachheads were secured, but any hope of advancing far inland proved ill-founded with the Turks holding the high ground armed with heavy artillery.

The ordnance supply ships proved too vulnerable to attack from shore-based artillery and their captains were unwilling to risk their craft. At Anzac, Forbes suggests that 'it was only possible to dump ashore such stores as were needed on the spur of the moment'.[5] At Helles it was possible to carry out the original plan in a more orderly way. Nevertheless, the decision was taken that both ships should return to Mudros.

Plan B was to supply direct from Alexandria; however, the distance proved too great to make this workable. The 40-mile trip from Mudros was thus selected as an alternative, with frequent sailings of small craft to the beaches.

The operation was supposed to be quick and decisive for the Allies; it turned out to be long and gruelling. The defenders had prepared their trenches before the attack. During 1915 the Allies constructed their own network. If you look at maps of the Dardanelles trenches, familiar names jump out. These were given to the trenches by their occupiers: Wigan Road, Oldham Road and, of course, Piccadilly Circus and Leicester Square.

The humour revealed by the trench names was in sharp contrast to the reality, or more probably a stratagem for mental survival.

With the shift to trench warfare, the number of men increased as did their armaments and even more so their demand for ammunition. The small craft simply couldn't cope and so a further, larger ship was fitted out as a further floating depot. This was the 12,000 ton *Minnetonka*, which had been fitted out for the transatlantic cattle trade. The *Umsinga* became her ammunition tender. Forbes' view on this arrangement is pretty unequivocal:

> It is impossible to imagine anything more utterly ill-suited for an ordnance depot than a floating ark. Time and again was the impossibility of running an efficient service from on board ship represented and the creation of a depot on shore urged.[6]

Major Man was for a number of months Ordnance officer on the *Minnetonka* when the demands on it had reached the maximum and Forbes records his contemporary description of what was going on:

> I remember one day in October when there were well over a hundred steamers anchored in the bay, dozens of which held stores, ammunition and clothing. We were desperately hard pressed for machine guns which were being telegraphed for from the front. The bills of lading told us that there were machine guns on board two or three different ships, but it would take weeks to get plans of the holds and find out exactly where they were stowed. Our parties therefore would board a fully loaded 4,000-ton tramp steamer and unload on to its deck hundreds of tons of cargo to find machine guns or whatever it might be. After a cargo had been overhauled in this way two or three times, one can imagine its hopeless state of confusion.

The next area of concern was due to the service between Mudros and Gallipoli being so uncertain. This meant that no one knew what was arriving and when:

> There was no time to clear the deck before a notification would arrive of some fresh departure. Before the end of the year the fore-deck was actually covered to a depth of from six to eight feet with stores which had been laid out for issue but not taken and which were so overlaid by later batches that they were never recovered for use and totally wasted.

The opportunities for theft by Greek and other working parties and by soldiers and sailors were unlimited. After a time, convoy-men accompanied consignments and matters improved a bit. But the unfortunate corporal or private found it very hard to protect articles strewn on the deck of a boat crowded with troops sleeping, sitting and standing, who had no respect for government property.

To keep accurate check was impossible and it is small wonder that, when accounts of the *Minnetonka* were eventually squared up, deficiencies such as 70 Vickers guns and half a million pairs of socks came to light.

I regard my five months on the *Minnetonka* as a nightmare. We worked as a rule seventeen or eighteen hours in twenty-four. The men were cooped up for weeks or even months on board and four of them went mad from overwork and worry.[7]

It became obvious that land-based depots were needed, however small and however inadequately equipped. Helles beach had been secured from the time of the first landings and a beachhead depot set up. Major Howell Jones was the DADOS to the 29th Division and he, with Major Teale of the Naval Engineers, achieved a measure of order. Teale addressed the ammunition shortage by setting up a local bomb factory making

Gallipoli HQ. (RLC Archive)

grenades out of jam tins. He also used his skills as a mining engineer to create an ammunition store some 70ft underground.

Anzac had proved vastly more difficult. At the start of the war the Australians had only just begun to set up an ordnance department and so they were lent the service of Major Austin AOD, who was the sole ordnance man to land at Anzac. Nevertheless, in time a dump was set up on the beach comprising clothing, guns and trenching tools. All seemed well until a 4.7 opened fire and 'great-coats, picks and shovels were dancing skywards'. The dump was moved to the other end of the beach where it was a little safer. It did, nonetheless, come under frequent shelling but was protected by a 'wall of clothing'. The Australians and New Zealanders were joined by Indian troops, whose only ordnance man was 'blown to pieces by a shell' on landing. Austin thus had to add the Indians to his care.

Hawkes' ship had arrived in the Dardanelles and witnessed heavy artillery fire until they landed some three days later. That was 4 May and Hawkes wrote of 'shells dropping all round our bivouac during night'. The next day he went up with supplies to the firing line, where he met many wounded and wrote, 'Passed in front of French firing line. *Rather exciting.*'

A month later, having been under fire almost daily, he wrote, 'Friday June 4th was a day that I should think that the Turks will never forget. About 10.30 a.m. there was a generalised attack on Achi Baba in which both the English and French fleets took part. He continued:

> It must have been awful to be on that hill where the Turkish position lay. The Allies' artillery simply poured shells into the hill while English and French ships were putting in an enfilade. The roar of the cannon was deafening and the hill was almost hidden by smoke.
>
> The rate at which we were firing was shown by 2 guns (18-pdrs, 90yh Battery K.G.A.) which put in 151 shells in under 2 hours. These two guns were just behind us and fired over our heads so we counted the shots. This bombardment continued until about 2 a.m. The Worcester Regt advanced and took five trenches.
>
> About 3.30 p.m. the first batch of prisoners were marched in and judging from their appearance they were very glad to get out of it. We also captured a Mohamadan priest and a miserable old creature he looked, as did two German officers. Two German sailors off the *Goeban* were also amongst the captured. They continued bringing the prisoners along in batches until Sunday. The average prisoner looked an awful poor creature.

Very dirty, frightfully old uniforms and generally like a very worn out British tramp. They are, however, men of big stature and I should think all or nearly all are well over 30 years of age.

From various accounts and my own observation this would have been a very successful day for us had we had reinforcements and more ammunition. But this is to all appearances a British failing viz: never quite ready. Were the Army officers or rather the 'heads' business men, in my humble opinion, the Turkish trouble would have been settled by now.

All day Saturday wounded were coming in and most units lost rather heavily. The 2nd Hants had only 42 left out of their battalion which was 1,000 strong when they came out.

Hawkes went on to write of more ordinary days and his duties as a Staff Quartermaster Sergeant (SQMS), drawing bread from the field bakery for all troops of the 29th Division about 20,000 men. He wrote of regular washing days and how many men became quite expert laundrymen. He then offered this account of a shelling he endured.

Saturday June 19th. There is no question that we have been more heavily shelled today than ever before. It started just before noon and for one and a half hours there was a perfect hail of shells. They fell all around us.

I at once made for my dug out, which by the way is only splinter proof not shell proof. As they fell they threw up clods of earth and then a hail of stones, bits of shell and humps of earth would fall on one's 'dug out'. You would hear the bang of cannon and then you would hear the horrid scream and whistle of the shell when it would make you hold your breath wondering where it would fall. Then a terrific bang when it exploded.

It was indeed a sickening sight after the bombardment as when we came out to see a number of poor horses that had been killed and wounded and were lying about. There were 16 poor beasts in a bunch, another 5 or 6 about 150 yards from my 'dug out', and in the horse lines in front of my home a poor creature had its shoulder blown off and yet it stood quite still. I think the sights of horses and mules wounded and killed affect one more than the wounded men.

Later in the afternoon we had another bombardment but this time not so bad or rather not so heavy. To say the least of it, the feeling and the sight at these bombardments are not pleasant. Some of the boys' faces turn quite white and there is nearly always that awful look of suspense as one never knows where the next shell will fall. You realise that you are face to face with death at such moments and these and senior ranks understand how necessary it is to put courage in the junior or young soldiers.

Were it not for the fact that some of the funny men crack jokes at these times our lot as senior NCOs [non-commissioned officers] would be very difficult.

It is clear that the job of quartermaster sergeant was not a back office role when he wrote, 'poor old QMS Leslie late QMS to 88th Infy Bde Hdqrs was killed during the advance. Five trenches were taken and a redoubt, also a battery of Turkish Artillery and a number of Maxims.' He then described how a 'shell fell at the door of one of the Royal Enniskillen's dug-outs and buried the occupant. After the shelling was over we crawled out when one of the men said, "I wonder if poor old Ned is in the dug out?"'

We at once commenced to dig and after about 5 minutes digging we came to some khaki and on touching it we found it was his hip so we dug away for all we were worth. Then we pulled the earth away with our hands and finally pulled the poor fellow out.

His heart was just beating, but after artificial respiration he died from shock.

Some days later this came even closer to home for Hawkes when he had gone to Gully Depot for supplies and saw the first two loads stacked:

Captain Gillam came up and seemed very upset and told me that 2 of my men had been killed by a shell soon after I left and one injured. After I had finished I rode back and got into camp about 1.30 p.m. and found 2 poor fellows who had been killed lying outside their dug out.

It was indeed a most awful sight and one I shall never forget. Pte Rigby had his head blown off and nearly all his bones were broken, while little bits of flesh were everywhere. Pte Crisp was not so badly blown about, but his face was black and it was difficult to recognise him. Pte Bowering had been taken to hospital but he has since died. Rigby and Crisp were two model soldiers and men I never heard grumble – both were married men.

Next morning, I had to see about their burial and this was done first thing. The thing I dislike most of all is searching and collecting dead men's things and sending them for despatch home. But a SQMS is expected to do and know about everything.

He wrote about further losses and then turned to the state of his own men:

My section is beginning to feel the strain of the campaign and I have now only 5 men of my original Supply Section of 12 left for duty, the others being either gone away sick or wounded. Poor Sergt [*sic*] Cooper and Pte Whitborne are very queer and not able to do much.

My men of the M.T. [motor transport] that are attached are in a very poor way and one has to be continually cheering the men, but half of them are not fit for duty. In fact, put all the men under my charge, *viz*: 51 now, together I do not think I could find more than three really fit men, yet it is wonderful to see how they go on with their duty and how little they complain.

On the 13th August I have to take over the remnants of the 86th and the remnants of the 87th Bdes which adds 4,000 men and 400 horses to my issue. I am now feeding about 8,000 men and 700 horses and mules with my little remnant of a Supply section and although I say it I think it is wonderful. I feel that with my men Sergt [*sic*] Cooper, Corpls [*sic*] Winyard and Whitten and Ptes Johnson and Whitborne I could do almost anything.

Gallipoli Suvla. (RLC Archive)

The diary records Hawkes' section being sent for rest and him being surprised and touched by the kindness shown to him. The rest didn't last long and his section joined the invasion at Suvla Bay. Here his job was at night to take water, which was scarce and had to be brought in by ship, to the troops in the trenches. All the time the men of his section were getting weaker.

The Suvla landings came after the summer and a very basic ordnance depot consisting of five tents was set up with ammunition stored in the open covered by bushes. The Suvla depot later came under the command of Lieutenant Colonel Hamilton, who wrote in his diary of the conditions being faced.

> One Friday afternoon we had a bad thunderstorm with a deluge of rain lasting some hours, then gradually, as the rain ceased, the temperature dropped and the wind increased. By the early hours of Saturday morning it was blowing a blizzard with an icy blast. It was bad enough to us in our indifferent shelter [built from ammunition boxes with tarpaulin roofs covered with sandbags], but it meant disaster to the troops in the trenches taken unawares, some sleeping with little on except shirts and overcoats. The first we knew of the state of affairs was the arrival of a continuous line of stragglers returning to the beach in the most pitiable state of exhaustion. The store-tents were emptied, straw was placed in them, and all available stretchers fetched. Rum obtained from the ASC and boiling water were used to succour the worst cases, but several men died from exposure. Then came the difficulties of dealing with the stragglers who continued to arrive throughout the whole of the next day. Two or three tables were placed on the beach, the bales of clothing were opened, and as the men filed past the necessary articles were issued to each. I think I am right in saying that, roughly speaking 8,000 men were evacuated as a result of this blizzard.[8]

Forbes states that the correct number was probably nearer 12,000 and adds this rather apologetic sentence: 'If for no other reason the Corps did at least earn the gratitude of the troops for having ample and early supply of good warm clothing landed on Gallipoli.'

Notwithstanding that it was no fault of the AOC, the difficulties in landing supplies must have caused dreadful problems for the troops. As elsewhere, there was a lack of ammunition. There were other shortages: trench mortars and sandbags. On the plus side, the campaign made

Gallipoli evacuation quay. (RLC Archive)

no great technical demands. There were few vehicles, no heavy guns, the largest being 60-pounders, and hence no complex ammunition. There was no gas, but there were far too few machine guns.

In October 1915 the decision was taken to evacuate. The plan demanded that any movements should take place at night and that dummy camps should be set up to deceive the enemy. The plan succeeded and over the next two months the surviving troops were taken to safety but not before enduring much further suffering.

Hawkes's diary continued briefly to describe the scene in December after winter had set in:

> I had a cup of tea and then I had to issue supplies to my Brigade and in a few minutes our Depot was one raging torrent and the night as black as pitch. It continued like this until about 9.30 a.m. but this time there seemed to be small rivers almost everywhere and we were often knee deep in water and slush.
>
> After getting all the carts away I came back to my dugout only to find that there was about 4 inches of water deep on the floor and everything was saturated, even my blankets. About 10.30 a very cold wind set in from the North and we spent anything but a pleasant night.

We made big fires to dry ourselves and keep ourselves warm.

Saturday turned out a terrible day and we were busy rushing up medical comforts, rum and dry clothing to the firing line. We hardly had time to get a mouthful or anything but felt that we should not stop at anything in order to get stuff up to the poor beggars in the trenches.

Up in the firing line they suffered very badly during the storm, a number were drowned while others were waist deep in icy water holding the trenches.

The Turks must have lost very heavily as they were in lower ground than we were.[9]

This description of the Gallipoli campaign is very much of glimpses from the point of view of the ordinary soldier. Martin Gilbert offers a telling observation from those in charge. Sir Julian Byng, who had led the 3rd Cavalry Division with Tom Leahy as his DADOS, took command of the British forces in Gallipoli in August 1915. He complained to General Hamilton about the lack of high-explosive shells. Gilbert notes Hamilton's opinion that Byng's experience on the Western Front had given him 'inflated standards', adding, 'that if he is going to wait until we are fitted out on that scale, he will have to wait until doomsday'.[10]

The ordnance activity at Gallipoli never really got organised. During the summer, salvage operations got under way and some equipment was recovered. With the evacuation, human beings were given priority, nonetheless much essential ordnance equipment was shipped back. Forbes reports that twenty-four store ships were needed to take everything back to Mudros.

As Forbes says, the fighting had been desperate and our losses very heavy without anything to show in return. He adds that:

although conditions of life were naturally much easier for the AOC than for those in the trenches, in no theatre did the Ordnance share so fully all the hardships of the campaign. In the cemeteries of Gallipoli are the graves of several of the Corps killed in action.

SALONIKA

Whilst the campaign in Gallipoli was under way, the Allies sent an expeditionary force to Salonika in order to save Serbia. It arrived too late, but for the next three years provided an influential presence in the region.

As with all accounts, it is down to serendipity as to what is recorded and what survives. Major Bernard Darwin, a well-known golfer and writer on golf, was a temporary officer and witnessed at first hand the setting up of the ordnance operation to serve the campaign.

Forbes recorded his opening summary, which rather sets the tone of what is to follow:

> There were not enough officers or men, not enough room, not enough transport, not enough labour and not enough stationery – this last a very important matter when any kind of storekeeping and accounting has to be established. Besides all these deficiencies there was one very serious surplus – mud.[11]

He continued:

> On the 26th of October 1915 there landed at Salonika two companies of the AOC, a small party having arrived a few days earlier from Mudros. This band of pioneers had its mobilization equipment, a little paper, a few pencils and for the moment no great amount of stores … the pitching of tents was begun by the dim light of lanterns on a night of drizzling rain.

The first small depot was no sooner set up than it ran out of space and a further depot was formed a little down the unmade road cut off from the first by the Royal Engineers' (RE) base park. A fleeting visit by Colonel Jackson from Alexandria caused yet a third depot to be formed on a nearby bare hillside; Darwin adds, 'recently ploughed'. The stores from the first two were to be transferred to the third, which would become the main depot for the campaign. This would have been an onerous enough task for the small AOC contingent, but by November supplies had begun to arrive in trickles and by December in an impossible flood.

The dock area was quite unable to cope and stores had to be stacked on public roads. The unloading of ships was hurried. Darwin gives the example of the *Stork* carrying tentage. The tents were unloaded but before the tent poles could be accessed, the *Stork* had been sent off to make way for a troop ship. The troops receiving the tents had to cut down trees to make their own tent poles.

To add to the chaos, the weather broke:

> The bitter Vardar wind brought with it a blizzard that raged for three days. Work was practically out of the question, and this incidentally at a time when some of the divisions had no winter clothing. Later again, in December, just at the time when the move to the third depot required the pitching of a number of store tents, a furious storm blew down the tents, exposed the stores to the gale and buried some of them forever in the mud.
>
> Such weather, of course, had a disastrous effect on the transport of stores from the docks, which could then only be carried by road. The road from Salonika to the depot was so bad that a lorry setting out from the docks one day very often didn't return until the next, and the digging out of lorries was a common occurrence. As to the roads in the depot itself, they were boggy and foundrous, and many of them of but a temporary character. Where evening had seen a road, morning would find a heap of stores covered with a tarpaulin that had sprung up like a mushroom in the night.

Amid the muddy chaos, pilfering and theft became yet another problem for the AOC men, who now found themselves detailed to sleep in the store tents to stem the losses:

> On the 9th of January General Mathew arrived [from France] as Director of Ordnance Services and it was only during the early months of that year that something like order had gradually evolved out of the chaotic conditions at the base Ordnance depot owing to the bad start made.

Three light mobile workshops had accompanied the division sent to Salonika and they were installed on the first site, only to be removed to the third. They lacked some essential equipment such as engines, dynamos and machinery and also corrugated iron sheds to hold them. It would be February before these eventually arrived. It was not until the summer that a site large enough to store 25,000 tons of ammunition was created with the essential laboratory facilities.

The lines of communication from base to the front were quite different from those experienced by Mathew in France. There, one railhead could service a division; here a whole range of different arrangements were needed to supply three divisions stretched over 60-odd miles from the sea up into the mountains. Some brigades were supplied by ship, others by rail and yet more by road. In time light railways were constructed.

Ingenuity was key. At one point no ink could be found; a temporary officer, a chemist, gathered together what was needed in order to make enough for orders to be written out. In view of the distance from the UK, any local manufacture presented savings. Soap was made from waste fat, of good enough quality for the French Army to buy. Verchoyle Campbell was COO Ammunition and used his extensive knowledge and experience to manufacture aerial mines to protect ammunition dumps from air attack. Gun inspections, which were normally carried out at mobile workshops, had to be accessed on foot given the mountainous terrain.

All these instances of initiative are admirable, but not necessarily the way to win a war. The ordnance operation at Salonika began disastrously and only got better very slowly. Like everywhere, there were flashes of normality such as the Christmas concert in 1916. The programme was signed by Colonel McVittie, who later came out of retirement in the early

Daimler mobile workshop. (Copyright Jaguar Daimler Heritage Trust)

Christmas in Salonika.
(RLC Archive)

Salonika 1916.
(RLC Archive)

years of the Second World War. His son was taken prisoner by the Japanese in Hong Kong[12] and later led the RAOC in the Cold War.

EAST AFRICA

> In December 1914, when I had been put in charge as DDOS with temporary rank, the local business community became anxious of the profits they had found so easy with an un-business-like local ordnance … So they surrounded me at the club bar one evening. Being aware how intensely they disliked me, this bonhomie put me on my guard and I spilt several pegs. They put it to me tactfully that it would pay me to work well with them in local purchase.[13]

This is just one short passage of one of several long letters that the 33-year-old Captain Routh of the Indian Ordnance Department wrote to Colonel Jennings, Director of Ordnance Services, in Simla. Jennings had selected Rouse for the posting during the East African Campaign in 1914–16. In September 1914 Routh had been detailed to proceed to East Africa with Ordnance Field Park 'B' force and to take over Ordnance 'C' force, Nairobi. The landing of B force had been repulsed at Tanga but had landed at Mombasa in early November 1914.

Routh took over as Assistant Director of Ordnance Services of the main line of advance a year later a hundred miles along the railway towards Moshi, the enemy capital on the south slopes of Kilima N Jaro, as they called it. He also organised the base depot at Voi for three divisions.

Routh's letters are both long and detailed, and it is clear from them that he was a true enthusiast for his work. In his letter of 26 March 1915, he wrote about ammunition supply:

> On one occasion I became aware that the General Staff were nervous about the 4-inch ammunition on Lake Nyanza having only 60 rounds. Application to the Admiral for a few more failed, so we cabled War Office to arrange. Two days later when in Mombasa, I saw the *Pyramus* of the Pegasus class, at anchor in Kilindini harbour, at which I got into a boat and called on the Captain. After the third gin he told me they were replacing 4 inch common by lyddite, so I persuaded him to give me 100 common and sent this off to the Lake by passenger train.

The day after returning to Nairobi, I was sent for by three anxious generals. Heavy fighting at the Lake, only four rounds of 4-inch remaining. Situation critical. What could be done?

They were very relieved to hear the 100 rounds had arrived. Where a senior officer would have overcome local obstruction by a strong line, I solved it by personal relations with the man.

A little later in the letter he turned his attention to machine guns:

One of the first things to do on arrival was to make the best use of such resources we had. This especially applied to machine guns in isolated posts, for which we managed to secure 40 obsolete .45 inch Maxims from India. Capt. Philips, 28th Punjabis was appointed by me as Divisional Machine Gun Officer, with two armourer sergeants to tour the country, and this remedy proved successful.

Routh then added this in parenthesis:

An interesting sequel to this was the arrival in 1916 of Commander Josiah Wedgewood MP for whom some suitable touring job had to be found. Philips was made Staff Captain while Wedgewood took on his job. I found that hence-forward Wedgewood's inspections depended on his political needs, rather than pure MG's [*sic*] and spares, and it was lucky that by then sufficient material was available to avoid a breakdown.

A letter of August 1915 is revealing of a quieter period when less urgent matters could be considered. The question of arming officers was one example. It seems that the .303 service rifle would be too heavy and so some .303 sporting rifles were found and issued, one per company. For gun inspection routines, Routh said:

We find many conditions approximating more to peacetime. Thus examination of guns has to be undertaken and I do so up to 6 inches. For all these things we should have an Armament Artificer, but such things, in the opinion of India and England, are not for us. Not so coffins, 'we store coffins for stock in all depots now, at great advantage to King George.'

Routh really does have a wonderful use of language with sentences such as these, opening long and involved paragraphs: 'Signalling in East Africa is interesting. Clear air and isolated hills give amazing possibilities'; or: 'The question of stores from England rather worries me, examining the W.O. [War Office] vocab as the Christian examines his Bible'; or 'There are those who consider Ugandan Railway less advanced that the Isle of Wight Railway.'

Moving away from Routh's letters, the bigger picture was of the eastern side of Africa essentially divided into three: one British, one German and one Portuguese. With the outbreak of war between the British and Germans, it was natural that their respective colonies would be drawn into the struggle. For the British, the governor already had at his disposal three battalions of the King's East African rifles; he had a police force and was able to muster one infantry regiment and one regiment of mounted rifles from settlers, many of whom were ex-services. As is clear from Routh's account, equipment was basic.

Colonel Scott had been appointed Director of Ordnance Services for East Africa. Forbes paints a revealing picture of the challenge that faced him in equipping the force. From the very start he, like everyone else, was faced with shortages of just about everything. Forbes makes the point that the fact that Scott knew personally many of the War Office departmental heads made his job a little easier.

The East African Force was made up of British, Indians and coloured troops (his words) and Scott had no real idea of what and how much would be required; it was likely, but not then certain, that the War Office would be equipping the entire force and not just the British. Scott gathered sufficient supplies for six months for 20,000 'white troops' and the same number of 'coloured' beside 4,400 white mounted troops.

Challenges there were a plenty. Tents had to be provided from India, and the Indian Ordnance Department was not keen about the arrival of the Brits, as becomes clear from this observation quoted by Forbes from Brigadier General C.P. Fendall's book on the campaign:

Some of them showed very plainly that they did not like it [the arrival of Scott and his staff] and it was natural that they should not, but there was no need to show it as aggressively as they did. What they disliked, as much as losing their places at the head of service, was being brought under

English ways of working in place of Indian. With the exception of these departmental officers, everyone seemed pleased with the change; glad that, at last, there was a chance of something being done, and that there was a staff in the country to cope with the work.[14]

The process of setting up depots continued, with main depots at Kilindini, Voi, Nairobi and Entebbe and four advance depots. Confusion prevailed for a good while between the various functions, with duplicate requests and materials arriving in the wrong place, although matters settled relatively quickly. The advance depots, though, had moved; the campaign proved to be highly mobile.

It was not just the amount and types of equipment that were to prove to be key to the campaign, but rather twin enemies of terrain and disease. The terrain and climate meant that transporting anything was difficult.

Richard Pullen wrote of the sheer variety of lorries that had been provided, British Napier engines and American four wheel drives (FWDs), quoting an observation made to him by Sergeant Harold Downs DCM of the 11th Hull Heavy Battery Royal Garrison Artillery. As seen even more sharply in the Second World War, the task of supplying the correct spare parts was a nightmare. In the end a decision was taken 'to allow the Napiers to run into the ground and concentrate on the FWDs'.[15]

Many places, though, were totally unsuited to wheeled vehicles. To begin with, pack mules and ox wagons were used. The tsetse fly proved more than a match for the oxen and thousands died. Next a large number of donkeys were ordered from South Africa and South America, and donkey pack saddlery was devised. Forbes notes that the donkey did not survive the tsetse fly for long enough to find out whether the saddlery was effective.

The third transport alternative was to scour the East African colonies for native porters and some 130,000 were found. They too were vulnerable to injury. Ordnance was given the job of providing the necessary packing case suitable for porter loads. Clothing for the porters became an issue. With protests from clergy and nursing sisters, khaki shorts were added to the brief equipment lists.

In August 1916 Routh was transferred to Mesopotamia at the request of the Government of India. From September 1916 Dar es Salaam became the main base depot.

4

THE SHELL CRISIS AND THE BIRTH OF THE MINISTRY OF MUNITIONS

On 26 May 1915 Lloyd George and a tiny staff began work as the Ministry of Munitions in a rather grand town house at 6 Whitehall Gardens. This house had once been the home of W.E. Gladstone, but more recently had been an art gallery. It became the home of 'the men of push and go'.

JUST HOW BAD WAS IT?

R.J.Q. Adams wrote an account of Lloyd George and the Ministry of Munitions.[1] In it he tells how, barely a week into its existence, Lloyd George's Parliamentary Secretary, Dr Christopher Addison, more than ably assisted by university economist and statistician Walter Layton, had produced a preliminary report on the armaments position. The report contained proof of such a dearth of supply that no copies were printed and even the Secretary of State for War, Lord Kitchener himself, had to come to Addison's office to read the draft. There was one brighter spot and that was on the supply of explosives. Early in the war, the eminent scientist Lord Moulton had been invited to chair a committee on the production of explosives and clearly this had already borne fruit. This was not the case elsewhere.

In relation to guns, there were enough 18-pounders, the most used gun, for twenty-eight divisions. The problem was that Lord Kitchener was insistent that some seventy-five divisions would be required. A slightly better story was told in the report in relation to 4.7in and 60-pounder guns, with enough for thirty-one divisions. The position with 4.5in and 5in howitzers was desperate, there being enough for only seventeen divisions. Very heavy artillery had not even begun to materialise.

The position in relation to rifles was no better, with only enough, at 538,000, for thirty-three divisions. With home output at 12,000 per week and overseas orders for 130,000, the War Office suggested that 1 million might be available by February 1916. As has already been mentioned, the position with machine guns was catastrophic with only enough for twelve divisions on order and a production capacity of one sixth of the estimated annual requirement of 26,000. The production of mortars was negligible and troops had resorted to making their own grenades.

Even if there had been sufficient guns, the supply of ammunition was only worse. The War Office estimated the need for forty-two days' supplies of shell in the Lines of Communication. The 6in guns were fully supplied, but there were only eight of them in the field. There were twenty-two days of 60-pounder shells, twelve days of 18-pounder and just over a week for smaller calibres.[2]

It can only have been to Lloyd George's immense frustration that, in spite of this quite extraordinary report, the War Office continued to resist the transfer of powers and activities to the new Ministry.

There is no record of what Lloyd George said. What he did, though, is on record. Dewar tells how he set out to the north-west to talk to armament and engineering companies to explore what might be done.

THE MEN OF PUSH AND GO

The Bill creating the new Ministry received the Royal Assent on 9 June 1915. On 16 June this Order in Council installed the new minister in his post:

> It shall be the duty of the Minister of Munitions to examine into and organise the sources of supply and labour available for the supply of any kind of munitions of war, the supply of which is in whole or in part undertaken by him, and by that means, as far as possible, to ensure such supply of munitions for the present war as may be required by the Army Council or the Admiralty or may otherwise be found necessary.[3]

Arguments over detail took time to resolve, but, by the time Lloyd George's own time as minister was drawing to a close in mid-1916, the Ministry 'controlled virtually the entire process of armaments production: from research and development, procurement of raw materials and machinery, supervision of both private and State factories, to the provision to the War Office of finished guns, shells and other warlike stores'.[4]

The way in which this was achieved is probably down to the manner and abilities of the man who came to be known as the Welsh Wizard. He said from the very start that what was needed for the job were 'men of push and go', by which he meant businessmen who got things done. One of the drawbacks of gathering a group of such people together was that the room would be filled by men more accustomed to giving orders than to receiving them. Lloyd George seemed to have a gift in managing such men, provided they did not run too much counter to his own views.

The essential structure of the new department was in place by 25 June with Sir Percy Girouard, formerly of the engineers Armstrongs, in charge as Director General of Munitions Supply. Under him were three deputies: George Macauley Booth was to deal with local organisation of munitions supply including labour and the ongoing collection of data. Eric Geddes, former managing director of the North Eastern Railway, headed up the production of artillery, and Glyn West, who had worked with Girouard at Armstrongs, was to manage the production of artillery ammunition, machinery and materials.[5]

Adams tells how this set-up lasted only to the end of July because of 'differences' between Lloyd George and Girouard. Girouard's position was eventually taken by Sir Frederick Black, a former Director of Navy Contracts at the Admiralty, who saw his role as the carrying out of the policies of the Minister, something he did with great effect, for 'he remained in his post until long after Lloyd George left the Ministry'.

Lloyd George ensured that his direct reports were men of proven administrative ability; only then could they have as their reports those with particular technical expertise. This essentially had been the core of his differences with Girouard. That Lloyd George's view prevailed was another significant factor in the effectiveness of the new Ministry.

In July 1916 Eric Geddes moved to be Inspector General of the British Expeditionary Force in France, following which he would take on the crucial role of Director General of Military Railways and Inspector-General of Transportation. He was replaced in the Ministry by Charles Ellis of the shipbuilders John Brown and Company. Leonard Llewellyn, of the Cambrian Coal Combine, became director of raw materials; Alfred Herbert, of the machine tool company that bore his name, had responsibility for machine tools; Ernest Moir of engineers, S. Pearson and Sons, took charge first of machine guns, and then of the Inventions Department; Vincent Raven, who had worked with Geddes at the North Eastern Railway, took control of the Royal Ordnance Factories; and the respected chartered accountant, Samuel Hardman Lever, became head of the Ministry's finance department.

The Ministry thus had in its senior ranks men of business with a proven track record of getting things done. The task, though, was vastly greater that any of them had undertaken before.

SETTING ABOUT THE TASK

The second task, following the gathering of data, had already begun with George Booth's activities at the War Office over the winter of 1914–15. Booth admired Kitchener and had won his trust, and with his agreement had formed the Armaments Output Committee. He also had the support of Lloyd George who, in due course, arranged for Booth's Committee to be attached to his own Treasury Committee.

Booth had been convinced that thousands of engineering firms around the country could convert their facilities to various sorts of armament

Guns en route. (RLC Archive)

production. This view was widely shared by the engineering businesses themselves, not least by a group of manufacturers in Leicester.

This particular group applied to the War Office for assistance and advice on how to convert their engineering shops for shell production. The Master General of Ordnance was not enthusiastic, but nonetheless arranged for Major-General Mahon to travel to Leicester on 23 March to meet with them. The Director of Artillery had different views and announced only days before the meeting that, contrary to this, no one from the War Office would attend and indeed no more contractors would be allowed until the labour needs of those on the War Office list had been fully met.[6]

Booth enlisted the support of the Secretary of State, the meeting was reinstated and the Leicester group became the model for local Munitions Committees across the country, or it would have done had Booth's and Lloyd George's Committee not been subsumed in the new Ministry. This gave Booth the power he needed to direct as well as to accept local initiatives.

Clearly there were a number of ways of skinning the munitions cat. There were, though, two core issues: the supply of labour and the availability of technical expertise. This latter point was held dear by the Master General and the military as a whole. For example, there was a reluctance early on to use American manufacturers since the USA was known for mass production, whereas it was Britain that held the torch for precision engineering. Military technical expertise was concentrated on Woolwich and those firms on the War Office list.

With the formation of the new Ministry, Booth was able to direct energy into his scheme and the Ministry recruited James Stephenson, managing director of distillers John Walker, as Director of Area Organisation. Stephenson divided the country into areas[7] and, building on the already existing area committees, set up boards of management for each. It would be through these boards that the Ministry could direct and control production.

Stephenson and Booth[8] conceived three models that areas could follow in their work.

Class A was the National Shell Factory scheme, where the state through the Ministry would finance the building of new factories, which would be managed by the board of management but with the Ministry holding the purse strings. Some fifteen areas opted for this route.

Class B was known as the Co-operative Scheme, whereby boards would contract with the Ministry to produce an agreed number of shells. Businesses would produce parts, which would be assembled in a board-managed facility paid for by the Ministry. Some eleven boards opted for B Class.

Class C was where businesses would simply contract to do the work with capital raised locally. Some seven boards opted for C Class.

The final twelve areas, including Manchester and Grimsby, opted for a combination of A and B.

The boards of management would have an area office with a representative from the inspection department at Woolwich, a labour officer and a superintendent. This network produced about a quarter of the shells, mainly of light and medium calibre, fired by the British Army.

There remained the issue of large-calibre shells, which were being demanded more and more as the opposing armies sought to shell each other into submission, or at least to make them sufficiently vulnerable to infantry attack. Booth called together the larger armament companies and proposed the construction of national projectile factories that would, with the management and expertise of the armament companies, manufacture the necessary shells.

The final issue at that stage of the war was the filling of shells, where the capacity of Woolwich was being far outstripped. Here Booth proposed the construction of national shell-filling factories.

CHILWELL

Once again the key would be finding the right men of 'push and go'. One such was Godfrey, the 8th Viscount Chetwynd, as Lloyd George recalled:

> To help us with the problem of shell filling I had the good fortune to secure the services of Lord Chetwynd, who was recommended to me by Mr Ellis as the best man to help us in our difficulty. He had, as far as I remember, no practical experience in dealing with explosives but he had a tremendous store of resource and ingenuity. I was however warned that he was very sensitive to any attempt to control him by a bridle of red tape.[9]

This warning turned out to be entirely apposite as Chetwynd set about the task.

The first issue facing Lord Chetwynd was how to produce the required quantity of amatol in the quickest, cheapest way that would result in shells that would not be adversely affected by premature firing, or indeed non-firing. At the time there were two processes for the production of amatol. The first, the melt process, mixed 40 per cent ammonium nitrate (AN) with 60 per cent trinitrotoluene (TNT) into a porridge-like substance that was then poured into the shell. This compared with the dry powder process that ground and pressed together 80 per cent AN and 20 per cent TNT into a dry 'cake', which was then pressed into the shell. This latter process was slow but much cheaper.

Chetwynd visited the Curtis & Harvey works in Faversham, which supplied Woolwich, and found the dry powder process 'most primitive'. His letter to Addison continues and then we begin to sense the type of man Chetwynd was:

> Those present consisted of people who, I was told, were experts on the subject. Before much had been said I had direct confirmation of their ignorance of the whole thing and was appalled at the position, the simplest and most ordinary laws of nature being completely disregarded.

The bit was now firmly between Chetwynd's teeth and he set to work to explore mixing processes being used elsewhere and importantly with similar substances such as flour and sugar. He therefore visited Brunner,

Mond and Company at Northwich where ammonium nitrate was manufactured and also Tate's sugar factory at Silverton. His diary entries of his visits speak of a man more given to action than words.

He had previously set out the criteria for the ideal site for a shell-filling factory. It had to be located between the shell manufacturing factories, most of which were just north of Nottingham, and the port of embarkation. It had to be away from large areas of population. It had to be wooded. The reason for this was that filled shells could be stored and, if explosions occurred, the trees would break their force. It had to be in easy reach of the railway network and, if not on top of large populations, near enough to the available labour force and accommodation for those workers whom they would need to bring in. The then villages of Beeston, Attenborough and Long Eaton proved perfect.

The site having been identified, Chetwynd wasted no time in identifying and approaching the land owner and acquiring the site. He then set about getting around him the key men he needed, the major pieces of equipment and engaging London builders, Holland, Hannen Cubitts. The digging of foundations began on Sunday, 13 September 1915.

The Treasury, which was of course footing the bill, naturally requested copies of drawings. The poor officials must have been driven to distraction, as a later article in a Glasgow newspaper stands witness:

> He planned the factory on half a sheet of newspaper and when the Treasury wired, 'must see plans as soon as completed'. He wired back, 'Factory half-built; will send plans as soon as completed'.

Albert Hall of Vickers was appointed chief engineer. It was at this point that Chetwynd and his team bumped into the world of shortages. The men of push and go were beavering away on the many tasks that Lloyd George had demanded. One result of this was that suppliers of just about everything were at full stretch. One example of this was the provision of electricity and so a temporary generating plant was found and installed.

The core issue, though, remained: how was the problem of mixing amatol to be resolved? Chetwynd continued his visits to manufacturers and continued his diary entries. 'I must say I was horrified with the whole place,' he wrote of the firm Leitch & Co. The issue this time was TNT and how it could be mixed at speed without reaching dangerous temperatures. The answer he found at British Dies Ltd of Huddersfield, which was processing TNT 'in a form in which some 50 per cent to 60 per cent would pass through a 60 mesh sieve'.

It seems that this sowed the seed of the idea of 'grinding and milling the amatol mix into very fine powders'[10] and Chetwynd went ahead and built on the Chilwell site his own experimental mill for grinding TNT. Concurrently he was still examining the process of grinding ammonium nitrate and found that in order for it to retain its powdered state it had to be kept moving; this resulted in a decision to install a continuous con-veyor belt from the AN Mill at Chilwell to the Mixing House.

Then on 7 September 1915 a very large fly landed in the ointment. A document marked SECRET arrived from Major Strange at the Ministry that cast doubt on the whole idea of an 80:20 dry mix, which, so Strange asserted, would result in far too many non-detonations. Chetwynd's reaction could be guessed: 'I asked definitely whether I was to stop or go on, as I declined to go slow.' It transpired that the concerns had arisen from the experience at Woolwich where shells were being filled from pressed 'cakes' of the 80:20 mixture and that this was result-ing in premature explosions.

All looked bleak until fate lent a further hand. Chetwynd heard that a commission was leaving for France in mid-October 1915 to look at, among other things, the French method of shell filling.

Chetwynd was convinced by what he saw and rapidly revised the design of the factory to employ the French method. From that point it was full steam ahead through the cold and mud of the awful winter in 1915–16, and by March the first shells were being filled. The construction task had been massive: 6,000 tons of constructional steelwork, 80,000 tons of concrete and 10 million bricks. The site had its own railway system. It filled most of the shells thereafter fired on the Western Front.

In March 1916 Frank Perks, my maternal grandfather, was still commanding 9 Platoon, 18th Middlesex Regiment Pioneer Corps, using the skills he had learnt from his father, who then ran the Long Eaton building firm of F. Perks & Son. On 19 April his commanding officer wrote a letter of recommendation for home service and he was appointed to the position of shift superintendent in the Chilwell melt filling department; a job for which Lord Chetwynd wrote he had great trouble finding the right man. Later in November 1917 Frank was promoted to supervisor of the melt shop, where he served until it was closed with the Armistice.

Melt house. (RLC Archive)

In the early part of the factory's service, it was the experimental mill and what became known as the old melt house that turned out the filled shells ready to be taken by rail to the front. These buildings were soon replaced by a press house for filling smaller calibres and the new melt shop for larger shells. The volumes were vast. Essentially all the shells fired during the Battle of the Somme came from Chilwell, enabling the British to 'match and even outmatch the German artillery'.[11] By 1 September 1916, 1 million shells had been filled, rising to an astonishing 19 million by the time the Armistice was signed. Hundreds of trains would come and go with their lethal loads.

In the beginning the factory relied on a few male civilian workers supplemented by a labour corps battalion. This latter was replaced by 1,000 attested men brought up from London under the scheme run by Lord Derby. Later, as the army demanded more and more men for the front, women joined the Chilwell workforce.

Emma Wyles, who worked in the press house, recalled the dust-filled environment and how she and her fellow workers had to wear cotton wool respirators for 'the fine yellow powder of the amatol was everywhere'. Those working directly with the TNT or the amatol mixture quickly became recognisable away from the milling houses because being in such close proximity to the TNT resulted in their hands and faces taking on a strange yellow hue. The yellowness soon became the trademark of the 'shell fillers' and Emma Wyles recalls that they were called 'the Chilwell Canaries because of our hair being yellow'.[12] It wasn't long before the dangers of shell filling became clear, with cases of toxic jaundice that proved fatal unless the affected women were removed from contact with the amatol.

There were accidents, including a number of fatalities. The welfare supervisors also became anxious about the workers' general health, particularly of the women; they were becoming malnourished and this did nothing to encourage full production. The answer was for the factory to provide two canteen meals per day in exchange for a 10 pence deduction from wages.

Frank Perks kept a number of memos from Colonel Sir Neville Chamberlain, Chilwell's danger superintendent. One from 26 February 1917 warned factory supervisors of a preparation used by Independent Workers of the World for setting fire to premises. It was clear that, with Chilwell fulfilling such a key role in the war effort, those seeking to disrupt it would see it as a key target. The description of the preparation was attached:

> The preparation consists of a small round clear glass bottle about one inch in diameter and three inches long, containing a small stick of phosphorus about one and a half inches long and about the thickness of a knitting needle, also a small quantity of liquid together with an ounce of cotton waste.
>
> The liquid is a mixture of turpentine and carbon bi-sulphide containing phosphorus in solution.
>
> With the cotton waste is occasionally used some small thin strips of celluloid. The solution is then worked into the cotton waste and into the form of a ball. The material is dropped in a position where, when it ignites, as it does after evaporation spontaneously, it may set fire to any favourable material in close proximity.
>
> It was in this way that several large warehouses were recently destroyed in Sydney at a cost of £500,000.[13]

The whole workforce was told to look out for cotton balls amongst the piles of waste.

On 1 July 1918 an explosion tore through the mixing house and killed 134 workers, only thirty-two of whom could be positively identified as the remainder were beyond recognition. A further 250 were injured.

Lord Chetwynd's 10-year-old daughter later recalled the event:

> I was startled and fully expected to receive a scolding for being out of bed but instead my father walked across the room, cuddled me in his arms and with a warm kiss on my forehead turned round and left without saying a word. I instinctively knew that something was terribly wrong.[14]

It had been a massive explosion but the other workers on site rallied round to help the injured and they were joined by men and women of the neighbouring villages.

The impact on Chilwell was enormous, but the very next day all fit men and women reported for work. It is clear from a letter that Lord Chetwynd wrote to Frank Perks that the melt shop took much of the strain and, not only was production not stopped, but it actually reached record levels in September to supply the final advance. The explosion was talked about even in Parliament, where the Parliamentary Secretary for the Ministry of Munitions coined the phrase Chilwell VC, a phrase that stuck. It is probably true to say that the cause was never found. Some suspected sabotage but this was never proven.

Shell-filling factories were formed all around the country, in Woolwich, Chilwell, Glasgow, Liverpool, Leeds, Banbury, Morecambe, Pembrey, Abbey Wood, Horley, Devonport and Hereford. Factories producing cartridges were established in Woolwich, Glasgow, Liverpool, Leeds, Gloucester and Hayes; and for making fuses and tubes in Woolwich, Perivale, Abbey Wood, George Kent, Bickford, Smith & Co., Thames Ammunition Works, Southwark, Hayes, Elswick, Coventry and Cardonald.[15]

Elsewhere as the war progressed, the Ministry would arrange to manufacture or would contract for heavy artillery, gauges, optical glass, shell steel, lumber products, anti-personnel chemicals and many other warlike stores.

Towns and cities throughout the country joined in the war effort. Coventry claims a particular place in this.

Chilwell explosion. (Perks Archive)

COVENTRY

Coventry's official handbook written shortly after the war said this:

> It is safe to say that no English city was so completely absorbed in
> munitions production as Coventry … It was not merely a question of
> adaptability of existing facilities. New factories sprang up in such numbers
> and on such a scale as to change the whole face of the city in the matter
> of a few months. New suburbs grew up like mushrooms, thousands of
> strangers of both sexes flocked to Coventry from all parts of England in
> answer to the call for munitions.

Hotchkiss produced 50,000 machine guns, Hillman Motors made shells
and recruited women for its women-only shell plant. Standard produced
aeroplanes. In 1915, the Coventry Ordnance Works employed 6,121 men
and 1,341 women and Daimler 4,750 people producing ambulances, staff
sleeping cars, motor lorries and, with Fosters of Lincoln, tractors for the
haulage of 4HE howitzers.[16]

Coventry had sixty-two government-controlled or owned establishments that together produced 300,000 tons of munitions; the Coventry
Ordnance Works alone produced 40,000 tons including sixty-six heavy
guns. Daimler put out 100,000 tons of shell castings. Some 800 new
houses and hostels were built.[17]

Another Ministry of Munitions factory, No. 10, was the Holbrook
National Filling Factory just outside Coventry. It was operated by
White & Poppe, who had been engineers in the city before the war
manufacturing petrol engines for Singer and Morris, for narrow gauge

Shell factory. (RLC Archive)

railway locomotives and for Dennis Brothers' vehicles including fire engines. In 1914 their workforce numbered 350 men. Work on the shell fuse filling factory began on 21 March 1915 and it began production in the November of that year with the first ten women employees being sent to Woolwich to learn the techniques required. By the end of 1916 the number of women had increased to 4,000 with 800 men; by the end of the war there were 12,000 people working on site producing both fuses and detonators. As with Chilwell, the women suffered a yellowing of their skin.

The factory was not near to a large available working population and so girls from elsewhere were brought in and were accommodated on site in specially built hostels and cottages bordering Holbrook Lane. A whole range of facilities were provided: three canteens capable of turning out 36,000 meals a day, with 100 acres devoted to vegetable growing with some seventy gardeners; an open air swimming pool and recreation ground; a 350-seat cinema; a hospital, an ambulance and fire service.[18]

White & Poppe produced a magazine for its employees, entitled *The Limit*, which cost two pence. The first edition appeared in July 1918 and contained an article called 'Aspects of Factory Life', with the strap line 'Women Labour'. Some short extracts offer a flavour:

> Many thought the advent of women unaccustomed to regular work was an experiment foredoomed to failure, as it appeared to them that the enthusiasm of women would evaporate, and their value therefore decrease.
>
> Women of all types came to work on munitions, some accustomed to the routine of shops, others who had worked in offices, small businesses, or in service, and yet others who had not done anything for a living.
>
> The motives which brought them in were many and various, stern necessity, patriotic zeal, and the craving for a new experience were among their number.
>
> In the early days the critic of women had many chances to ride his hobby. Caprice, a charm in leisure hours, was a cause of trouble in well-ordered factory systems, lack of mechanical sense again clogged the wheels and diminished enthusiasm threatened to justify carping criticism.

The conclusion was 'It's dogged as does it: the gained doggedness of women, directed by intelligence will win this war.'

Doggedness, though, could not emerge victorious on its own; other deep-seated issues needed to be tackled.

LABOUR

As early as March 1915, the Master General of Ordnance had declared that the biggest contributor to the shortage of armaments was a chronic lack of skilled labour. This was in complete contrast to the expectations of the government that on the declaration of war there would be a drying up of demand and that mass unemployment was probable. Little did they know the massive demands that the requirements of modern warfare would place on industry.

A number of different reasons for the labour shortage were identified and an equal or greater number of attempts were made to address them, both before and after the creation of the Ministry of Munitions:

- The very existence of the War Office list of approved suppliers meant that the geographical areas from which skilled labour could be found were themselves restricted. Workers could not readily move.

- The call to the colours drew many skilled men who wished to fight for their country. It was estimated that in 1915 around about one fifth of eligible skilled men had joined up. Recruiting sergeants were in no hurry to turn away keen recruits.

- Workers in munition factories were not uniformed and so, if young and able bodied, would be the recipients of white feathers from such as suffragettes.

- Industrial relations in the years before 1914 had been strained. Unions were fiercely defensive of the privileges of skilled workers and would resist any suggestion that men, or, heaven forbid, women, possessed of lesser skills would be allowed to work alongside unionised skilled men. By the same token, unions were highly suspicious of employers making profits from war work and so would not cooperate willingly.

At the heart of just about each of these issues revolved the degree of control that the government should have over employers and workers. From a standpoint of a century later this may seem odd, not least when placed alongside conscription under the Military Service Act of 1916, the consequences of which for far too many conscripts was death.

A number of initiatives were taken to address the issues:

- The position of munition workers being handed white feathers was eased by the issue of badges first by the Admiralty and then, but in far fewer numbers, by the War Office. Badges could be ignored, and indeed were by at least some recruiting sergeants.

- A number of voluntary schemes were set up that would allow skilled workers in effect to volunteer themselves to serve not as soldiers but with their hard-earned skills.

- Ministry of Munitions legislation provided encouragement to skilled workers to move where they were needed.

- Efforts were made to release from the army men whose skills could be better used in munitions production. Such efforts, though, met with resistance not only from the army itself, but also from the men in question, who did not want to walk out on their mates.

- Attempts were made to identify men in non-government supplying industries whose skills could be redeployed. A registration was carried out in mid-1915 and some redeployment took place, but the real result was confirmation that the skills simply were not there.

In addition, calls went out to the Empire and to foreign countries. Empire employers resisted, preferring to receive orders for armaments rather than demands to release workers. In terms of foreign countries, Belgium was top of the list, since some 100,000 Belgians has sought refuge in Britain in the early months of the war. There were skilled men among the refugees but attempts at integration were not successful. Belgian-only factories were set up and one in particular at Elizabethville was in a newly built Belgian-only town.[19]

Shell factory workers. (RLC Archive)

The core issue, though, was the closed shop, as we knew it in the mid-twentieth century. Unions were determined to protect skilled workers; employers were reluctant to take on a fight. Yet, step by step, with a good many reversals en route, the principle of dilution – the taking on of unskilled men and women to work alongside skilled men – began to grudgingly be accepted.

The situation faced by the Scottish engineering company, Beardmore, discussed in Chapter 2, is illustrative of much of this.

Such events stiffened the resolve of the government, which seriously considered 'taking possession' of the companies on the War Office list. It relented, but on the advice of the respected accountant Sir William Plender, proposed a restriction on the profits of armament suppliers as a quid pro quo to the unions relaxing restrictive practices for the duration of the war.

THE ROLE OF WOMEN

Restrictive practices, the refusal by the unions to allow non-skilled labour into their factories, truly revealed itself when the likelihood emerged of many women entering the workplace. Before 1914 only about a quarter of the adult female population had employment. Of those, most were in domestic service, nearly as many in the textile industries and comparatively few in commerce, so 'shop girls', and even fewer in government service, mostly teachers. The idea of women working in engineering was unthinkable both for male employees but also for employers. In much the same way that government had feared mass unemployment as a result of war, this was so much more so with women, whom they feared, having lost their man, would become reliant on the state. This remained the case for the first year of the war as the government tried to find, for those who wished it, employment.

The armaments crisis changed all that and a very strong demand for labour was clear for all to see. But could it be filled by women? Could they do the work? What would happen in workplaces where men and women worked side by side? Would they need to be paid the same? Before 1914, women earned around about half of their male counterparts. Notwithstanding the efforts of the suffragettes, the place of women in 1914 was still in the home.

The movements that would result in a great many women entering the workplace began slowly. In the autumn of 1914, the Board of Trade did make some efforts in placing some women in the War Office list factories but the number was only about 2,000. In March 1915 labour exchanges opened registers where women could record their interest in munitions work; the take-up, though, was still small at 79,000 by June 1915. Smaller still was the number who were actually found work:1,816.[20]

The message that could be gleaned from the magazines of the time was that women should do what they had always done but with greater economy; spare time should be spent knitting for the troops. It is worth stating too that even nurses were being rejected by the War Office in those early months.

The suffragette, Mrs Pankhurst, was probably the one person who could unblock the jam that this clash of views had created. On 17 July 1915 she led a march of some 30,000 women demanding the 'right to serve'. She, with a few others, met with Lloyd George and it is worth repeating what she was reported as saying to him:

The women in this procession to-day have taken part because they wished to demonstrate their desire to serve in any and every capacity in which they may be of use … We do urge that wherever a woman is engaged like a man, she should be paid the same rate of wages, whether she is doing piece-work or she is engaged in what is called time work.[21]

Lloyd George accompanied her back to the crowd and said this:

The Government will see that there is no sweated labour. For some time, women will be unskilled and untrained, and they cannot turn out as much work as men who have been at it for some time. Therefore, we cannot give the full rate of wages. Mrs Pankhurst is quite right in insisting that whatever these wages are, they should be fair, and there should be a fixed minimum, and that we should not utilise the services of women to get cheap labour.[22]

Adams suggests that Lloyd George, 'had no idea in July 1915, that his guarantee of a fixed minimum would require his new department to set and enforce wage rates for millions of female and unskilled male dilutees for the entire war'.

The debates over wages kept the labour department of the Ministry fully occupied for many months. The end result, though, was that women were both attracted into munitions work and, albeit reluctantly, accepted.

The reluctance dimmed as more and more women took their places in the factories and showed to their employers and male colleagues just what they could do. Reports to the labour department, one held in the National Archives entitled, simply, *Dilution*,[23] told of women working as oxyacetylene welders, operating drill presses and lathes turning out bands for 4.5in shells, manufacturing helical gears on huge milling machines and machining gaines that detonated fuses in artillery shells.[24]

The principal article in the June edition of the *Ministry of Munitions Journal*[25] was devoted to 'Women's Work on Munitions', leaving the reader in no doubt as to its effectiveness. The magazine was produced from December 1916 for the benefit of organisations attached to the Ministry. It contained a variety of articles, a good number of which were on welfare issues but with the bulk being quite technical pieces on equipment, processes, workshop practice and armaments.

The number of women entering factory employment adds further evidence of the success of the Dilution scheme:

July 1914 to July 1915	382,000
July 1915 to July 1916	563,000
July 1916 to July 1917	511,000
July 1917 to July 1918	203,000[26]

By 1918 very nearly half the workers in government establishments were women. The addition of such numbers of employees into factories, especially those dating from 1914 and earlier, posed problems of working conditions. There were inadequate sanitary facilities, and there were inadequate places for eating and rest during breaks. Some work, especially for those handling TNT, was damaging to heath. All this prompted Lloyd George to appoint the reform-minded industrialist B. Seebohm Rowntree to take on the role of leading a new welfare section of the Ministry. In this role, Rowntree reduced excessive working hours. Under his oversight some 700 canteens were introduced into munition factories, health policies were introduced and sanitation was much improved.

Welfare supervisors were introduced into workplaces to ensure that the conditions under which women worked were adequate. Some philanthropic provision went further. Under Rowntree's influence some employers built houses and temporary hostels for their new employees; in other cases, the Ministry itself provided accommodation. Having said this, the figures quoted are a fraction of the number of women actually employed and so it would be fair to assume that for many crowded and inadequate housing was the reality.

WOOLWICH

The process of transferring functions from the War Office to the Ministry of Munitions must have appeared like a third front upon which the war was being fought.

The question of control of the Royal Ordnance Factories at Woolwich, Waltham Abbey and Enfield was one that Lloyd George was originally content to leave on one side, with the Master General of Ordnance in control. As the months went past, the situation showed no signs of improvement; the stacked up wagons full of shells awaiting filling being the most visible. Lloyd George tried first persuasion but, when this failed, he went to the Cabinet and in August 1915 finally persuaded Prime Minister Asquith that control had to be transferred to the Ministry. Lloyd George recalled the moment in his *War Memoirs*:

When I took over Woolwich I soon found why, in the words of M. Albert Thomas (his French opposite number), it was '*une vieille boite*' ... [Those in charge] jostled each other, they were in each other's way, hindering but never hustling, and only acting together when there was any resistance to be offered to the political Hun … My first duty was not exactly to lay these ghosts but to put them in their proper places; to see that each of them pushed his own trolley without running into anybody else's. I saw why we had been delayed in diverse ways.[27]

His response was to bring Woolwich and the other factories within the remit of Eric Geddes and then to appoint Vincent Raven, another railway man, to the office of chief superintendent.

Von Dunlop, in his defence, questions just how quickly these changes yielded results, pointing out quite reasonably that 'no complete round made and filled under the orders and arrangements of the Ministry was supplied until early April 1916'.[28]

WEAPONS DEVELOPMENT

The development of weapons was the final area of battle between the War Office and the new Ministry. Adams is entirely clear that the War Office, principally under von Dunlop, simply was not doing the job. He cites fuses. The method that had been employed for years by Woolwich was resulting in too many prematures with the consequent loss of life as the guns exploded. The French had adopted a revised system that was not only safer but also quicker and cheaper. The War Office, it seems, had its head in the sand.

To counter this, in part, is Dewar's contention that if the army ever needed anything it need look no further than Woolwich since, if they didn't yet have it, they would make it. This evidence of expertise he supports further by his suggestion that Woolwich men were a source of skilled advice for the whole armaments industry.

This again is perhaps countered by the evidence of the advances made by at least some of the War Office list firms, the rail-mounted big gun for example. We could add to this the whole development of the machine gun by Vickers.

The story of Chilwell adds yet more evidence. Adams writes of thousands of empty shell cases waiting outside Woolwich, which it was completely unable to fill at anything like the same rate that the cases were being produced. This was in the context of an army desperate for shells. The result of Chetwynd's efforts was a process that was many times faster than the Woolwich way.

Was this evidence that the War Office way could simply not keep pace with the demands of modern war? Whatever the truth, the result was a turf war between the Ministry and the War Office that lasted some nine months.

Von Dunlop's 1919 paper, outlining his defence to the criticism levelled, pointed out, on the subject of prematures, that the difficulties could easily have been resolved under his department.[29]

We have already noted the reluctance of the Director of Artillery to accept the proposal by the group of Leicester businessmen that armaments could be made by any suitably equipped and trained engineer. It was the Director of Artillery, along with the Master General of Ordnance and his Ordnance Department, who was entirely clear that it was only soldiers who could possibly know what weapons the army required. They were in touch with the fighting troops. They had all almost certainly served with regiments in the front line of action. We have seen that Ordnance officers were not only experienced soldiers but had also undergone a seven-year 'apprenticeship' before becoming fully fledged. This surely gave the War Office solid grounds for its assertion.

To counter this again, there was the evidence coming from France. Sir John French, Commander-in-Chief of the BEF, had set up an Experiments Committee under the chairmanship of Major-General Sir John DuCane to examine suggestions for new and improved weapons being put forward by the officers and men of the BEF. Lloyd George's memoirs record a letter written by DuCane to his friend, Colonel Arthur Lee, the then Military Secretary to the Ministry of Munitions.

I am pretty sure that you will find that the system by which the War Office and the Ordnance Board retain responsibility for these [design] matters is your great stumbling block. The MGO's people seem to me to be mentally exhausted and the Ordnance Board and the Experimental Department at Shoebury to be hopelessly congested.

K's great argument for keeping control [of munitions design] was that he must be responsible for the safety of troops … He has failed hopelessly as regards safety, and the result of his control now is to prevent the causes of the trouble being definitely ascertained.[30]

The process under criticism was for the army to place a request, for the MGO to supervise development and, once approved, to make available plans and gauges to enable production. Adams suggests[31] that the principle adopted by the MGO was that, on the declaration of war, all development ceases and all efforts are put into production. This principle proved to be fatally flawed.

The net result of these further factors was a clear view on the part of Lloyd George that experimentation and development also had to be transferred to the Ministry. Once again this was easier said than done. Kitchener himself was resistant as, of course, were the Master General of Ordnance and the Director of Artillery. Adams suggests that Prime Minister Asquith sent his Secretary of State for War on a trip to the Eastern theatre simply to remove him from London and to give Lloyd George a chance to get a grip on the development issue. It worked, and in late November 1915 Major-General DuCane was appointed Director General of the first Department of Munitions Design in the Ministry of Munitions. This transfer reduced the role of the War Office to:

> The Duty of fixing the requirements of the Army both as regards the general nature and amount of the munitions required, together with the duty of allocating such materials, and the Duty of receipt, custody and actual distribution of all such supplies.[32]

If Lloyd George had thought that was an end to the matter, he was destined to be disappointed for there remained the School of Musketry at Hythe, which was in reality a testing facility. It was not until 1 February 1916 that this was eventually transferred to the Ministry.

That still wasn't all. There was also a small War Office Inventions Branch, A41, and the Admiralty under Winston Churchill had created its own Armaments Committee to work with the Royal Society. With the creation of the Ministry, the then First Lord A.J. Balfour recommended a joint approach. It will hardly surprise that the War Office was not enthusiastic.

The Ministry set up its own Munitions Inventions Department under E.W. Moir, who had previously worked with Eric Geddes. This department soon discovered that it was in effect in competition with A41. The final decision in November 1915 drew a line under this and placed the whole business of army munitions invention under Moir.

The twenty-third report of the Munitions Inventions Department, dated 10 August 1917[33] and addressed to Winston Churchill as the then Minister of Munitions of War, offered a review of its activities in the first two years of its work. It was under the name of Colonel Goold-Adams, who took over from Moir in December 1915, when Moir was sent to work on ordnance supplies in the USA.

The report talks of the 34,114 inventions of which it received particulars. The advisory panel had 32,321 cases under review and of these 2,565 were sufficiently promising to justify further research. The report then refers to an annexure that lists twelve that were both adopted and considered important. These included a tool for a Lewis gun invented by Sergeant Harrison, the Claudsley's hydraulic buffer (for guns) and Jakeman's sound locator (for mining). From reading elsewhere I can immediately see the usefulness of these. It wasn't always the case.

The report highlights a number of drawbacks in its processes and these include a lack of reference to the actual needs of the army. The list of those involved in the department as advisers includes many eminent engineers and scientists and I wonder just how much of their time was wasted and how they were viewed from the front.

SOM (M) E GUN !

AOC workshop review. (RLC Archive)

Nevertheless, Moir and his team became massively busy and, before Lloyd George left the Ministry, had examined some 14,000 ideas.[34] Probably the most innovative idea was the tank and this is discussed fully in Chapter 6.

THE STOKES MORTAR

The Stokes mortar was, in contrast to the tank, a weapon of great simplicity, replacing as it did the need for a rifled barrel, a breach or trigger; the bomb was simply dropped down the bore and this would activate its firing, greatly increasing the speed of fire compared to the howitzer and other trench weapons. Three bombs could easily be in the air at once.[35] An article thus describing the Stokes mortar appeared in the *Ministry of Munitions Journal* of May 1917.

Whilst the weapon might have been simple and a wonderful example of this inventive adaptability, its journey from inventor to soldier was tortuous in the extreme. Wilfred Stokes, chairman and managing director of Ipswich engineers Ransomes and Rapier, had come up with the idea and demonstrated it on 2 February 2015. The Director of Artillery turned it down. Stokes demonstrated it again, only to be told by the director that 'in view of satisfactory trench howitzers now in France and the fact that this makes another form of ammunition it is not proposed to adopt the design'.[36]

The records in the National Archives reveal intense frustration. Captain Lister took charge of the Stokes Gun Section of the Trench Warfare Department on 7 July 1915. He described the Stokes gun as a 'crude affair but [which] showed promise in view of its lightness, cheapness and rapidity of fire'.[37] The shell had a 12-bore sporting cartridge inserted into its base as a propellant. This use of sporting ballistite would prove an additional advantage when supplies of conventional howitzer propellant were running short and no one was prepared to release any for the Stokes project. Indeed, Captain Lister himself had to design an alternative to the 12-bore cartridge in order to achieve the range that was being demanded.

Of greater frustration was the experience of Lieutenant Sutton, a civil engineer, who had lost his right hand in Gallipoli and was invalided home.[38] He arrived in England on 12 June 1915, armed with a letter from General Hunter Weston asking for a supply of efficient trench howitzers. Sutton met Stokes and was duly impressed. Further meetings took place with Churchill and Lloyd George and further demonstrations, including to Sir Douglas Haig. All were duly impressed. There followed further meetings and enquiries into minute points of design. Sutton was reprimanded and in effect demoted for the fuss he was causing. Nonetheless, 300 Stokes guns reached France by the end of January. The evacuation of Gallipoli meant that they were too late to assist in the campaign that had cost Sutton his hand.

It was clear that frustration reached the level when humour became the only release and in the Archives there is a poem,[39] 'The Stokes Gun – An Epic'. Each verse mimics a traditional rhyme, for example:

Ride-a-cock-horse to Banbury Cross,
Send Stokes guns the Channel across,
Two hundred wagons with horses and men,
Then the plan changed and we all start again.

Not only was the Stokes mortar easier to operate, it was far cheaper and quicker to manufacture. It was not until Lloyd George himself placed an order from funds provided by the Indian Maharajah that the weapon was brought into use. It was then seen by the new Commander in Chief of the BEF, Sir Douglas Haig, and the rest is, as they say, history. It significantly added to the armoury of the British soldier.

PROJECTING NEEDS – THE DARK ART OF PROVISIONING WRIT LARGE

The Ministry of Munitions took hold of the whole question of projecting the needs of the army into some sort of plan for the supply of weapons. Sir John French and others were entirely clear that the British Army needed a great many more pieces of heavy artillery. This would be the case for Kitchener's ambition of seventy-five divisions. Ministry men thought further ahead and made calculations for an army of 100 divisions. The results were terrifying. Yet, if the war was to be won, the tools with which to do the job must be provided. The numbers far outstripped the capacity of British industry and so the muscle of the Bethlehem and Midvale Steel companies in the USA was called into play. This is discussed further in Chapter 8.

Closer to the everyday needs of the soldier in the trench was the supply of grenades, which had been thoroughly neglected with the result, already mentioned, that soldiers would improvise with food cans and all sorts. The shortage became particularly apparent at Gallipoli.[40] General Sir Ian Hamilton, Commander of that Expeditionary Force, wrote, 'anything made of iron and containing high explosive and detonator would be useful. I should be greatly relieved if a large supply could be sent … as the bomb question is growing increasingly urgent'. The message was received on 9 July 1915. Within seven days 25,000 grenades had been 'loaded, packed and dispatched to a steamer that was taking cargo to the Dardanelles'.[41] The manufacturers were not on the War Office list, but their effectiveness was clear.

TECHNOLOGY SHORTAGES

An Englishman wanting a good pair of binoculars would buy a Carl Zeiss from Germany. Once a state of war existed between the two nations everything changed; Britain would need to become self-sufficient, at least among the Entente nations and neutral countries such as the USA and Sweden. To be dependent upon a German manufacturer for optical instruments was no longer possible and optical instruments would be needed in a large variety: gun sights, telescopes, periscopes and camera lenses for aerial photography, to name but a few. In the case of glass there was a further, rather large, problem: potash, the essential raw material, was mined in Germany but was only found in small quantities in Britain.

In the early autumn of 1914 the immediate need for field glasses was met by a public appeal.

In 1915 the situation was becoming critical and the Ministry of Munitions took hold of the issue and set up an optical munitions and glassware department.[42] It engaged the services of the much smaller existing British optical glass industry, including Chance Brothers of Birmingham and Ross Ltd, whose small factory was just off Clapham Common.

As with so much of this story, human ingenuity came into play and two chemists, Mr Chance of British Cyanides and Mr Leigh of the North Lincolnshire Iron company, experimented to see how potash could be produced. It was found as a by-product of iron ore, by the introduction of salt into the blast furnace.

The third element of a solution was training in order to fill the skills gap. Some of the firms undertook this themselves but there were also institutions such as the Northampton Polytechnic Institute in Clerkenwell that 'would put girls through their paces'. This was definitely an industry where even men believed that women could carry out the precise processes every bit as well as them.

Another area of at least equal seriousness was the need for precision engineering to produce and test the many thousands of gauges that were needed in armaments production. At the start the issue could be and was dealt with by Woolwich which, after all, at that point produced all the plans and measurements.

In the case of gauges, it was to the National Physical Laboratory, an offshoot of the Royal Society, to which the government turned for help. In 1915 the laboratory had a staff of five men testing 1,000 gauges a week. By the end of 1917 the number being tested was more than ten times as many and by the time of the Armistice the number of testers had increased to 200.[43] The *Ministry of Munitions Magazine* of March 1917 contained an article illustrating the uses of gauges as manufactured by Brazil, Straker and Co. Ltd of Bristol.[44]

A third key technology was that of the magneto for motor vehicles, and that is explored in Chapter 6.

CONCLUSION

The Ministry of Munitions saw no fewer than four ministers during its First World War years, including the two greatest war ministers of the twentieth century: David Lloyd George and Winston Churchill. The Ministry and the men of push and go moved mountains. Without them the result of the war might have been very different. Nevertheless, it was one thing producing the weapons; it was quite another getting them into the hands of the troops who were to use them.

5

TRENCH WARFARE ON THE WESTERN FRONT

The role of Ordnance on the Western Front was vast: equipping millions of men with everything from a pair of socks to 18in guns. There were base depots both for stores and ammunition. There were workshops at base but also in lorries at the front. There were supply trains and railheads. The front was a latticework of trenches, tracks and narrow and broad gauge railway lines. There was, though, ordinary life too.

The subject too is vast and so in this chapter I try to paint a picture of the Ordnance machine using extracts of an unpublished account written very soon after the war by J.S. Omond, an Ordnance officer at the sharp end of Ordnance work and whose description of Woolwich opened Chapter 2.

Omond left Woolwich in the late autumn of 1914 and spent some months at a home Ordnance depot, which he does not name but at which the pace of life seems to have been relaxed. He was nonetheless getting impatient:

Happy though life at the Depot was and comfortable as home conditions were, the natural wish of every right-minded man was to be up and doing, so as to get overseas as soon as possible. This wish seemed unlikely to be realised as the months slipped by, and it seemed as if nothing would come of the aforesaid recommendation [Omond had been recommended for a posting to a division]. Inspectors of Ordnance Machinery and other officers came to the Depot and departed triumphantly for various theatres of war. Later on letters came from them describing what they were doing and seeing. The battle of Loos was fought in September, and the New Armies – the first hundred thousand of imperishable memory – had fought their first great fight with a valour which surprised many of the soldiers of the Old Army.[1]

On 20 September 1915 he received orders to report to Aldershot as he had been appointed DADOS to a division bound for France. In Aldershot he found a sense of bustle and urgency similar to that which he had experienced at Woolwich:

Units drawing stores in every direction, and in every sort of service pattern of vehicle so different to the cranky old civilian carts bought in the early days of the war more in haste than in prudence, so long as the wheels revolved. Here were mess carts, G.S. [General Service] wagons, maltese carts and limbered wagons, all bent in the one errand of going away with as much clothing and as many stores of all sorts as they could carry. Motor lorries and steam tractors abounded everywhere.

It was not until 14 December 1915 that Omond's division set off for France:

It was a frosty morning when 5.30 a.m., time to get up, dress, breakfast and be ready to start by car at 6.30 a.m., came round. Punctually at that hour a Sunbeam – one of the new cars to go overseas with DHQ [Divisional Headquarters] – reached the door.

Omond was a member of the advance party that was to find billets and see to the renumbering of the cars with the registered numbers they were to bear during their official life in France:

Boulogne was full of English soldiers of every unit, and British Military Police controlled the traffic. There were many nurses and endless motor ambulances were bringing the wounded and sick down to the hospital ships in the harbour. The town was very much anglicised and the shopkeepers made great endeavours to talk English, with varying degrees of success.

The journey from Boulogne was along relatively clear roads through countryside that was largely unaffected by war. He remarked on the road being macadamised before its surface changed to 'pave' ,never to be forgotten by the BEF for its greasy surface precarious to man, animal and vehicle alike. They passed through Bethune, 'a town dear to the hearts of many Englishmen on account of comfortable billets, baths, a theatre, an excellent tea-shop and shopping facilities'.

> It was indeed a haven of rest to war-weary men from the real front, and was as yet but little damaged by the fury of the tempest raging without its gates. The Hotel de France enjoyed a flourishing business until July 1916, when a bomb was dropped one fine summer's afternoon into the little square just outside the main entrance to the hotel smashing all of its windows … after that episode M. le Patron decided that discretion was the better part of valour, and retired to a more salubrious neighbourhood.

Reading Omond's account, there is no mention of fear or indeed excitement. The approach to the front witnessed a change:

British Western Front at Nesle. (RLC Archive)

The roads became more congested with traffic of all sorts. The roads and pavements dirty and unkempt, the houses falling into disrepair from want of care, and the inhabitants living a quite abnormal existence. Still further forward war conditions became more and more obvious. Troops were closely billeted in that area, and numerous houses must have contained many more people that they had been made to shelter … The soldiers lived in barns. Sleeping on the floor. Straw was used for bedding when it was obtainable. Their meals were served out of 'dixies' (camp kettles), the midday stew being poured or ladled into their mess tins. In one billet, these mess tins were placed on the ground amidst all the litter of a dirty farm-yard while each man's portion was given out to him. They remained cheerful and uncomplaining as ever, and laughed and joked as if they had never been accustomed to feed in any other way.

The division was reaching the stage where all the months of training would be put to use in anger. One or two of the points he records make the reader pause. 'Long Gum boots reaching to a man's thigh were allotted in certain numbers to each division for use in the trenches.' These were passed on as divisions withdrew for rest and were replaced. 'Latrine buckets were thrust on us by Corps Headquarters and braziers were sent up from base by the hundred.' The mention of braziers witnesses the extreme cold of that winter and the winds that on one occasion were strong enough to blow over six railway wagons.

Notwithstanding all of this, Omond's time at Divisional Headquarters was 'the best five months I had in France'. It is difficult to reconcile this with the events he records:

One fine morning towards the end of April 1916, at about 5 a.m., I was awakened in my billet by an orderly with a message to say that a gas attack was in progress … what wind there was came from an easterly direction. Presently a greyish white cloud drifted into the streets shrouding every house and tree like autumn mist. From my office, which was on the first floor of the school, it was possible to look down almost on to the top of this cloud.

Anti-gas helmets had arrived from Brigade and were loaded on the only available lorry to take up to the front. Tragically the infantrymen were so incensed by the 'Boches' attacking with gas that, charging at the enemy, some tore off their helmets and breathed in the full strength of the poison gas, going to 'their deaths, killed by the foulest and most treacherous weapon the devilment of mankind had ever invented'.

He goes on to describe a visit to the field ambulance on the morning of the first attack.

> This ambulance had its pitch in a disused brewery, on which much time and labour, paint and whitewash had been expended to make it a fit place in which to receive the wounded and the sick. There was a useful yard where motor ambulances could come and go; a petrol store, a pack store and all the various accessories which made British Field Ambulances into such wonderful improved hospitals. Nothing was ever left undone which would add to their efficiency and usefulness. In the midst of the buildings which formed the brewery, was a small courtyard. Under the shade of a projecting roof were several stretchers in a row.
>
> On each stretcher lay a victim of Kultur. Besides each stretcher knelt an RAMC [Royal Army Medical Corps] orderly doing what he could to assuage the agonies of dying men – dying quite literally from want of breath, strangled in the full glory of their youth, cut down like thousands of others as remorselessly as the gardener cuts down a weed, because of the insatiable greed and unparalleled cruelty of the German people.

Omond adds, 'and yet there are those who would forgive and forget'. He then talks about the great lengths taken to care for the animals in the field, the presence of a veterinary section and horse shows that took place between units. This sense of ordinary life is also evident from Omond's recollection of dinner parties in the period before the division entered action, and also the entertainments offered to the troops:

> Cinemas, variety entertainments, and concert parties were a constant source of joy to the troops. They were always well-attended by all ranks. The Y.M.C.A. had a hut near D.H.Q. which was the scene of many an excellent concert. I do not remember seeing anything but men among the performers in the advanced areas. They usually included a conjurer, who did many of the old familiar but ever welcome tricks which recalled children's tea parties, and a violinist who always was certain of a warm reception. Divisions and Corps were responsible for the management of the Variety Entertainments Parties, some of which visited London theatres.

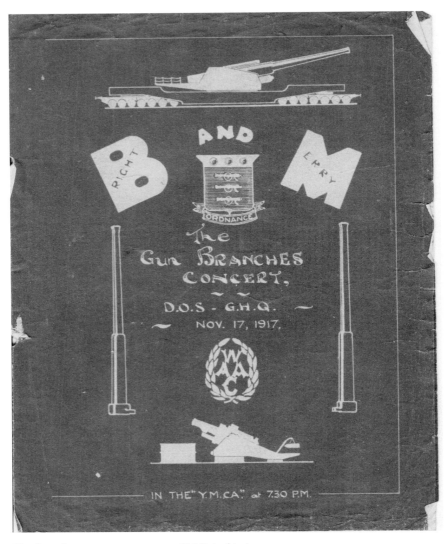

Gun branches concert programme. (RLC Archive)

There were other aspects of ordinary life: baths and laundry, the supply of which fell to Ordnance men. In the early days in Bethune baths were taken in wine casks. Shirts and underwear were handed in to be washed and repaired and clean replacements issued. The view, not far from Divisional Headquarters, also gave a sense of the ordinary, but so close to war:

Its easterly end dropped abruptly to a valley where the French army had seen some of its hardest fighting early in the war. To the south, lay fine rolling agricultural country dotted here and there with church spires, and the roofs of houses and cottages. To the north, lay the industrial regions of Northern France.

At right angles to the spur, that is from north to south, lay the trenches. There, visible to the eye, and expanded like a chess board, were communications trenches, gun pits, railways, shattered houses, coal mines and their attendant slag heaps, the crassiers, which will be remembered as long as the generation that fought there survives. But not a sign of a living man, woman or child.

It was almost uncanny because these trenches were filled with living men, living in the ever constant presence of death. Every now and then an aeroplane would wind its way across the line. In any instance, the sky would be flecked with puffs of smoke from the ever ready anti-aircraft

Postcard sent home whilst on a rest period. (RLC Archive)

guns. Or again, a great cloud of black dust and yellow smoke would rise from the ground, showing where some shell had come to rest among the slag-heaps.

Up on the hill top, no noise was heard. It was all as beautiful as a lovely Sussex down. But, nevertheless, it was a vision of the greatest of all the battles of mankind.

Omond's day-to-day role was to ensure that his division was supplied with all it needed from boots and uniforms to guns and camp equipment. He offers some description of his duties, which demand of him a high degree of accuracy to ensure that precisely what is needed is received. It is probably for this reason that his description relating to guns may sound to us just a little bureaucratic:

> Guns, Howitzers, Machine Guns and Trench Mortars, all form a very important part of a DADOS's job. It is up to him to see that any that are destroyed by the exigencies of the campaign e.g. by mine explosion or enemy fire are replaced at the earliest moment after he is acquainted with the necessity for their replacement.
>
> Supposing a Lewis Gun is buried in a mine explosion. The Battalion concerned should notify the DADOS at once of the fact, by wire, and up the gun will come. DADOS has a complicated wire to despatch to get the gun. First of all, it has to be in code, and, secondly, it has to be repeated to Corps and Army Headquarters, to Headquarters of Ordnance in the Field, and also to Q.M.G., G.H.Q. When the new gun reaches DADOS, he has to report its arrival to the Corps and the Army. That system also applies to Vickers guns.
>
> As regards Trench Mortars, and all nature of Artillery proper, the procedure is rather different, and introduces yet another Officer of the Ordnance Department, the Inspector of Ordnance Machinery. The I.O.M. is an expert in Trench Mortars and Guns as well as many other things. Before a new Gun can be demanded from the Base, he has to give his authority for its replacement. It amounts to this, that he goes to the Gun, examines it, and if, in his opinion, it cannot be repaired in his workshop, he instructs the DADOS to demand a new Gun.

Behind the divisions and corps and armies to which they belonged there was a support infrastructure of some magnitude. At the top, GHQ was described as the War Office in France. Under GHQ there were

Guns for repair. (RLC Archive)

some five armies each comprising a number of corps made up of a number of divisions.

From an ordnance point of view, at GHQ there was a director of Ordnance Services, an office held by Major General Harold Parsons for most of the war. Each army had a deputy director of Ordnance Services, each corps an assistant deputy director and each division a DADOS. Leahy makes the point that by 1916, when he was addressing the new staff officers on their Cambridge course, most DADOS were temporary officers and although able required the supervision and guidance of the regular and more experienced officers at army and corps level.[2] The article on Leahy's retirement underlined his credentials. He served as DADOS in France until October 1915, when he moved up to become ADOS Southern L of C and then 1 Corps and XV Corps until he was invalided to hospital in September 1917.[3] He was later posted as a member of the British Army mission in the USA. After the war he became chief ordnance officer on Gibraltar, having in his command one Bill Williams, who would lead the RAOC in the Second World War.[4]

Supporting this structure were the Lines of Communication, which had taken on a more formal structure, one North, under Colonel Heron based at Montreuil, and one South, under Colonel Scott, based at Abbeville.

For Ordnance there was then the network of depots, which would receive supplies from England and issue them to the divisions; as the war dragged on it was more than this, for the depots would also receive back from the divisions equipment that had been salvaged. This equipment might be repaired in the depot workshops or, if necessary, sent back to England for more major repair.

The main depots were at Calais, for the 1st, 2nd and 3rd Armies and units of the Northern Lines of Communication, and Le Havre, for the 4th and 5th Armies, the Cavalry Corps and the units of the Southern Lines of Communication. Le Havre was also home to a depot for guns and vehicles. The depots were each under the command of a chief ordnance officer who had reporting to him an Ordnance officer responsible for the depot's stores and a Chief Inspector of Ordnance Machinery, who ran the workshops.

The workshop operations at both Calais and Le Havre were very substantial establishments. Tom Leahy describes the make-up of the Calais workshops, covering 22,000 sq. yd. It was directed by the Chief Inspector of Ordnance Machinery. Under him were three assistant inspectors, an assistant inspector of armourers and a boot inspector, who together supervised some 700 artificers and tradesmen and nearly 600 women labourers. In the gun and carriage shop there were seventeen artificers, 100 fitters, two pattern makers and three moulders. In the armourers' shop there were forty-six armourers and twenty-one cycle fitters, and then eighty-two blacksmiths with seventy-eight hammer men, eighty-two carpenters, twenty-six painters, fifty-two saddlers, twenty-four tentmakers, twenty tinsmiths, sixty-three wheelers and seventy-six store men.

Most of these trades were also represented at divisional level. Each regiment would have its armourer, who would become largely redundant when the regiment went into action. As a result, divisions would group trades together where that led to a more efficient overall unit. A good example of this was in boot repairs; indeed at Calais, there was a boot repair shop some 500 strong.

The workshop network evolved to meet the needs of a war where materiel had become king. The experience of what might be termed 'big gun warfare' was wholly new. In the South African war guns had

Boot repairs. (RLC Archive)

consumed ammunition on a scale that was then unprecedented. Yet in the autumn of 1917, the British Army might use in one day as much as was fired in the thirty months of the South African war. Forbes gives some numbers. In the last three months of 1914, 7,131 tons of ammunition had been shipped and it had all been used; at that point the army was living from hand to mouth. In the autumn of 1917, in the operations at Passchendaele the equivalent figure was 465,000 tons. In all some 5 million tons of ammunition was landed in France for use by the British Army.[5] Ammunition usage on that scale had an inevitable consequence for the guns that used it: they wore out. A system was developed to take measurements to assess the speed of wear and so the programme of replacement. Worn guns also needed repair, often in situ, to keep them firing.

At the start, each corps was allocated a mobile workshop to carry out essentially minor repairs to guns close to the front. These proved so necessary that an additional workshop was provided to each corps. Each workshop would be run by an ordnance mechanical engineering

A Thornycroft J Type mobile workshop proves its worth helping to repair a field gun in France 1917. (Richard Pullen)

WORKSHOPS LEAGUE
Positions of Teams on Nov 4th

TEAMS	Played	W	D	L	Gls for	Agst	Pts
1. Storemen	3	3	0	0	8	3	6
2. Saddlers	3	2	1	0	10	2	5
3. Carpenters	3	2	1	0	9	4	5
4. Fitters	3	1	2	0	7	3	4
5. Depot	3	1	1	1	4	3	3
6. Armourers	3	1	1	1	3	3	3
7. Shoemakers	3	1	1	1	3	3	3
8. Smiths	3	0	2	1	5	8	2
9. Wheelers	3	0	0	3	2	10	0
10. T.P.T.	3	0	0	3	0	12	0

AOC Workshop Gazette. (RLC Archive)

officer with twenty-one other ranks and comprised a lorry fitted out as a workshop with machine tools and a stores lorry.

The arrival of heavy howitzers in March 1915 triggered the creation of heavy ordnance mobile workshops, which were allocated at army level according to gun numbers. These were bigger, with two officers and in due course up to 200 men including civilians. The following year, a third level of mobile workshop was created at corps level to cater for the ever-increasing number of heavy guns. The final part of the gun jigsaw came in 1917, by which time supply had caught up with demand, when gun parks were created to hold reserves.[6]

By the end of the war there were some sixty-five workshops employing 3,000 people who maintained more than 10,000 guns.

There was a separate *AOC Workshop Gazette* published with regular items such as the football league tables between the various trades.

The way in which the AOC was viewed by soldier and civilian alike seems to have been a live issue in the First War as it was in the Second.

In the first issue, an article appeared under the authorship of Lieutenant Colonel Everett that first set out to give an impression of the scope of work of the corps but then the sort of people who served. In it Everitt quickly set out to dispel the misconception that the corps was only about the supply of ordnance, that is cannon and firearms. He explained that the list of items that the army obtained through the AOC extended to 850 pages, to which must be added a further 400 pages for clothing obtained from the Pimlico depot. Items were divided into groups and he gave the example of leather, harness and saddlery. They were further subdivided and this, he explained, accounts for the rather cumbersome vocabulary used. The example he gave is of a cold chisel that, he said, had to be ordered as 'Chisel, hand, cold, one'. I remember as a child that my parents used to joke about this.

The editor of the *Gazette* went on to make a point about the type of person who served in the AOC. The example he gave was of a 'one-legged man' [of whom tragically the trenches had provided many] who volunteered and who was offered a position in the AOC. From the tone of the article, it is clear that the AOC did not wish to be considered made up of anything other than fully able-bodied men. The 'one-legged man', Everett suggested, would have been a clerk, adding that even clerks had to do a 'lot of running about'. He concluded that at any depot it would only be 1 per cent of roles that could be suitable for such a man.[7]

This is indeed a hot potato and very much of its time, as we now know from the Invictus Games and other accounts of today's soldiers with disabilities following full and fruitful lives. Not so then; it was clearly a sore point, since everything indicates that able-bodied men, without the other skills the army and the country needed, were sent to the trenches.

A later edition offered 'Army Commandments – in France':

The Colonel is the only boss, thou shalt have no other Colonel but him.

But thou shalt make of thyself many graven images of officers who fly in the heavens above, of Staff Officers, who own the earth beneath, and of submarine officers who are in the waters under the earth. Thou shalt stand up and salute them for the CO, thy boss will visit field punishment unto the first and second degree on those that salute not, and shower stripes on those that salute and obey his commandments.

Thou shalt not take the name of the SM in vain, for the CO will not hold him guiltless that taketh the SM's name in vain.

Remember that thou shalt not rest on the Sabbath day. Six days shalt thou labour and the seventh day is the day of the CRE [Commander Royal Engineers]. On it thou shalt do all manner of work, thou and thy officers, thy non-commissioned officers, thy sanitary men and the Kitchener Army that is within thy trench.

Honour thy Army Staff that thy days may be long in the Corps Reserve where one day they may send thee.

Thou shalt kill only Huns, slugs, lice, rats and other vermin that frequent dugouts.

Thou shalt not adulterate any section's rum rations.

Thou shalt not steal – or at any rate be found out.

Thou shalt not bear false witness in the orderly room.

Thou shalt not covet the ASC man's job; thou shalt not covet the ASC man's pay nor his motors, not his wagons, nor his tents, nor his huts, nor his billets, nor his horses, nor his asses nor any other cushy thing that is his.

Alice Morris June 3 1916[8]

Leahy also underlines the scale of the other depot work. Each of Calais and Le Havre handled some 15,000 separate items. In a four-week period the two main depots would issue: 45,500 jackets, 63,000 riding breeches and trousers, 52,000 puttees, 56,000 pairs of boots and 310 tons of horse shoes. Le Havre would issue 3 million sandbags each week.[9]

Forbes looked at a different period, ten months of 1916, and focused on the issues of rather different items: 11,000 prismatic and magnetic compasses, 7,000 watches, 40,000 miles of electric cable, 40,000 electric torches, 3½ million yards of flannelette, 1¼ million yards of rot-proof canvas, 26,000 tents, 1½ million waterproof sheets, 12,800 bicycles, 20,000 wheels, 5 million anti-gas helmets, 4 million pairs of horse and mule shoes, 447,000 Lewis gun magazines and 2¼ million bars of soap.[10]

These figures illustrate both volumes and variety. An absolutely key role in a depot was that of provisions officer. It was his job and that of his team to estimate how much of each store item would be required in the next month and then to place orders with Woolwich.[11]

Certainly in the First World War, but also in the Second and since, officers have been dealt with quite separately in that they would buy their own uniform and many items of equipment. With so many officers in France, the AOC set up officers' shops that would stock for sale all an officer might need. Forbes gives a figure of 12,900 for the number of separate visits to the Calais shop in this ten-month period. In due course a cashier from the paymaster's office was posted there.

These main depots would be staffed by forty officers and around 1,000 men. There were four other main but smaller depots. As will be seen, Abbeville held a slightly particular role, being close to the advance depot for horse transport. There was then Étaples, which concentrated on supplying hospitals. In the south there was a depot in Marseilles and in Paris a depot totally focused on clothing.

PARIS CLOTHING

Clothing was a huge issue, not least the salvage, repair and reuse of discarded items. The War Office was at first resistant to the idea of reuse, but in 1916 relented and systems were set up. To give just a few figures, in the period from May 1916 to May 1917, nearly 13 million pairs of socks were received from England but 30 per cent were returned for reuse; of 6 million shirts, a quarter were recycled; of 5.5 million jackets, trousers and greatcoats nearly half were repaired and reused.

Following the winter of 1914–15, numbers of greatcoats, blankets and horse rugs found their way back to Le Havre, the better weather having made them temporarily redundant. Colonel Heron, DDOS Northern Lines of Communication, saw that, with drastic washing, disinfection and repair, they could be reused the following winter. To undertake this task, he approached the Paris launderers, Joly et Fils. They undertook a trial that proved satisfactory and were awarded a contract. The volumes were large and would become larger and so an empty warehouse was leased at Quai de Javel close to the laundry. A small Ordnance team was set up in Paris to oversee the work, which would become an annual event.

The London store, Debenham and Freebody, set up a specialist cleaning plant for sheepskin-lined coats, fur undercoats and leather jerkins. In due course some of the washing gave way to dry cleaning. In time it was found that repair work could be performed more cheaply in the AOC's own workshop and Paris couturiers were taken on. Techniques were developed to clean and dry trench gum boots.

In the course of the war, the Paris operation dealt with 10 million blankets, 3 million greatcoats and jackets and many other items, including 115,000 kilts. Forbes estimates that the operation saved some £8 million by not needing to replace dirty items. Forbes suggests that:

Clothing repairs. (RLC Archive)

Without these salvage operations, all the sheep farms of Australia and all
the cotton fields of America could not have produced the raw materials we
needed; nor, even had shipping been available to carry them to England,
could all the looms of Yorkshire and Lancashire have sufficed to weave
cotton and woollen goods for our armies and civil population beside the
Allies whom we clad.[12]

AMMUNITION

The supply of ammunition was a different story. Colonel Mathew,
as Deputy Director of Ordnance Services at GHQ had, in late 1914,
assumed responsibility for the supply of ammunition to the railheads
and beyond. There followed the period of months when the supply fell
far short of demand and a form of rationing was introduced to allocate
what there was in as effective a way as possible. Ammunition arrived
at Boulogne by ship and was then loaded on to trains for immediate
delivery to the railheads and thence to the units through the medium of
ammunition parks and divisional ammunition columns.

The division of the Lines of Communication between North and
South necessitated an additional port of entry and Rouen was chosen.
If possible, small quantities would be held at both Rouen and Boulogne
to cope with emergencies. With the advent of heavy high-explosive
ammunition in the summer of 1915, a new bespoke depot was created at
Quevilly, 4 miles down the river from Rouen. This was designed around
a carefully thought-out railway layout that would facilitate speed of distribution. It was isolated and so not at risk from air attack, hence no
special protective precautions were undertaken.

By Christmas of 1915 the word was that with increasing production from the new shell factories there could, in the summer of 1916,
be 100,000 tons of ammunition demanding storage. Accordingly, it
was decided to build a further depot, this time at Audruicq, to relieve
Le Havre on the Northern Line of Communication.

Plans progressed satisfactorily until 10 March 1916 when, on the
second train to arrive in Quevilly, a box of 4.5in ammunition exploded,
wrecking much of the depot and costing three lives.

Amazingly, a stack of 3in motor bombs into which shells were actually
flung by the force of the explosion failed to ignite.

Rouen ammunition depot explosion. (RLC Archive)

Shell lodged between ammunition boxes in the Rouen ammunition explosion. (RLC Archive)

The accident was investigated and new guidelines issued for ammunition storage. Forbes records that an attempt to follow the guidelines would have greatly reduced the total storage capacity and so AOD staff did the best they could. Some additional capacity was found: 15,000 tons of ammunition were stored in a sugar beet factory, that were empty until harvest.

Some 101,771 tons of ammunition were landed in France between 24 June and 23 July 1916 for the Somme offensive.

On the night of 20–21 July Audruicq was 'visited by an enemy aeroplane and placed out of action by one small bomb which wrecked the entire depot'.[13] The damage was devastating with one rectangular crater that 'could have docked a battleship' and another that 'would have served as a vent to a respectable volcano'.

Astonishingly, the accident did not interrupt supplies to the front, but it did set in hand a whole different approach that would extend to the closing days of the war. This is discussed later in this chapter.

ABBEVILLE

No. 8 Ordnance Depot was established at Abbeville and commanded by Lieutenant Colonel H. W. Fairholme.[14]

Each depot kept a war diary of its activity. The diaries were compiled monthly and show a narrative for each day of the month. Reading one month with the next, it is possible to trace the resolution of issues and the execution of orders.

Part of the diary keeping may have stemmed from a note from the Director of Ordnance Services to the COOs of Havre, Rouen, Boulogne, Abbeville and Marseilles suggesting that, with a view one day to the writing of an 'ordnance history of the war', records should be kept of the names of officers serving, all departmental orders, returns of numbers of articles issued and the scope of work carried out. Many of these records were destroyed by fire, but fortunately some remain.

The diaries I read cover part of 1917 and the whole of 1918 through to the post-war period when the clean-up got under way. The 1917 diary speaks of regularity, whilst as 1918 progresses it gains more of a sense of urgency. However, in January 1917 the then Captain Fairholme offered a reflection on the early days of the depot.

Wheelwrights. (RLC Archive)

He wrote that 8OD had opened on 7 December 1914 and had grown from twenty men into a separate company of 265. The main items issued were boots and clothing. Significant mention was made of the salvage and reuse of items of all kinds amounting to several tons each day. There was in the depot a reserve store of guns and limbers. Field guns were issued to armies by train and machine guns by lorry. Lewis machine gun issues had outnumbered Vickers, and the issue of 18-pounder guns far exceeded all others. In terms of mode of transport, 64 per cent went by rail and 36 per cent by road for the period from June to October 1915.

The other significant item in the report was the repair of smoke helmets. They needed to build to a capacity of 250,000 per month and so required hut accommodation for their dipping, washing, drying and packing.

Other repairs carried out included those to 626 vehicles. The term 'vehicle' referred not to those powered by internal combustion engines but rather to those drawn by horses or by hand. Some 1,385 wheels were repaired. Abbeville undertook this work, being close to the advance horse transport depot.

Abbeville played an important role in the Somme offensive as it was able to store relatively close to the front reserves of guns and machine guns.[15]

THE SOMME

On the first day of the Battle of the Somme, the 19th Division was part of III Corps and was to be in Corps Reserve for the first phase, with the 12th Division in Army Reserve and the 8th and 34th in the first attack on 'Z' day, 1 July 1916.

The 19th Division had been formed on 11 September 1914 as part of Kitchener's Second Army. By March 1915 the division had been clothed in khaki, rifles and machine guns had been issued to infantry and transport was formed. The division left for France between 16 and 18 July 1915. The Order of Battle is intriguing from an ordnance point of view, since it is not mentioned as such. There is a divisional headquarters, artillery, engineers, a signals company and a cyclists' company. There are three Infantry brigades, pioneers, ambulances, Army Service Corps, mobile veterinary section and a divisional supply column (of which I assume ordnance was part). In July 1915 the DADOS 19th Division was Captain W. Smith. On 7 March 1916 Bill Williams took up the appointment.

Major-General Tom Bridges had taken over command of the 19th Division on 13 December 1915. It was Bridges who introduced the 'Butterfly' as the division sign; it soon became known as 'La Division Papillon'.

From 13 October 1915 to 1 July 1916 the 19th Division 'carried out trench warfare of a more or less vigorous nature'. From an Ordnance point of view, it is interesting to note from the DADOS Captain W. Smith's war diary that on 17 October 1915 100 steel helmets were received. 'Steel helmets were then in the experimental stage and were found [to be] of such protective value that all troops were subsequently equipped with them. Their use, however, did not become general until 1916.'[16]

An onlooker described the breaking of 'Z' Day, 1 July 1916, the first day of the Battle of the Somme:

Even in the trenches the dawn of the 1st of July seemed calm and sweet, at least till the full chorus of guns opened at 6.30. The field on both sides of the line now dissembled under a soft mist, above which here and there a high spire or lofty tree peeped out.'

Just before 'Zero' hour the officers from Divisional Headquarters partook of the Sacrament.

At 6.30 there was a sudden roar, an awful rending of the comparative stillness, which left men dazed and with that helpless feeling which comes with an intense thunderclap; the final hour of intense bombardment had begun … Before the hour of attack arrived several mines exploded, and clouds of smoke were released as the hands of watches moved slowly nearer 'Zero'.

7.30

With almost as great a violence as when they had begun at 6.30 a.m. the guns suddenly ceased, long lines of khaki clad figures leapt from their trenches and began to move quickly across No Man's Land. Immediately the sharp barking of machine-guns filled the momentary silence as the guns lifted off the German front line, and in many places the advancing line of troops were almost swept away … [17]

That evening Major-General Bridges was called upon to take the village of La Boiselle, without which progress on the flank was impossible. Such was the confusion following the unprecedented carnage of the morning that no straightforward plan was possible. As Wyrall puts it, 'an extraordinarily difficult task now faced the 19th Division'.

It is not the purpose of this book to trace the progress of battle; however, the following order of the day was issued on 4 August 1916 on behalf of General Bridges:

The Divisional Commander wishes to thank all ranks of the Division for the way in which, during the last 10 days, they have upheld the best traditions of discipline and hard fighting. The Division leaves a name behind it in the Fourth Army which will never be forgotten.

The battle of the Somme is still unfinished, and every effort is being made to wrest the full fruits of victory from the enemy and to gain such positions as will seriously dislocate his defensive system.

To this end fresh troops are required and the 19th Division will take its place at once in the defensive line in order to release another division for the attack.

When this is understood by the troops, the Divisional Commander is confident that they will play their part ungrudgingly and that every individual will continue to put forth his best efforts in this critical period. [18]

General Bridges led the British Army mission to the USA in April 1917 to seek to persuade them to join the fight without delay.[19] He returned to the front on 19 June 1917 to lead the division in the battles of Menim Ridge and Passchendaele, with its slaughter on an unimaginable scale. Bill Williams was mentioned in dispatches on 9 April 1917 for gallantry and devotion to duty;[20] this date coincided with the redeployment of the division ready for the Ypres offensive and demanded long hours of work organising dumps and ensuring that the division was fully prepared for the fight ahead. Bill Williams served with the division until 27 November 1917, when he was promoted to major and appointed DADOS GHQ Italy.

The division went on through to the end. Following the Battle of Ypres in 1917, Major General Bridges was severely injured. Nevertheless, he wrote again to praise the efforts of his men. Wyrall adds:

> It should, however, be remembered always that in winning great success for their divisions, the infantry in the front line could not have done so had it not been for the splendid cooperation of all arms of the Division: the RA, T.M. Batteries, pioneers and RE, Signalers [*sic*], and medical units, were constantly in the shell-swept area. The services of DADOS and his personnel in replacing and repairing destroyed and damaged weapons and equipment during the operations were simply immense. The Army Service Corps and Veterinary Corps were invaluable.[21]

There is, in Bill Williams's archive, a handwritten letter to him from General Bridges from hospital thanking him for:

> the great services you rendered the division here since you joined. I am by no means insensible to all the hard work you have put in and am grateful to you for it. I hope the New Years honours will give you some recognition.

They didn't, but Bill was award the Military Cross on 11 January 1918 for devotion to duty.

Omond's life too was to change dramatically toward the end of August 1916. He was called to DHQ and told that, following a few days' rest, his division would be joining in the Battle of the Somme.

For Omond the days of rest were days of intense activity as the accumulations of five months had to be returned whence they had come.

For example, armourers' stores had to be returned for use by the next division, similarly laundry and bath stocks and underclothing.

The day for entrainment came and with it, for Omond, an excellent lunch at Hotel du Commerce; for the troops, a wait in the pouring rain for the train to be made ready. Yet, 'it was all in a day's work, and everyone was in the highest of spirits at the prospect of a change of scene, and of taking part in the then greatest battle in which the British Army had been engaged'. In spite of the wait in the rain, 'the French railway authorities and personnel had made a name for themselves on account of their wonderful methods of handling troop-trains, and their patience and willingness to help and advise both man, beast, and vehicle that day were noteworthy'.

> All along the side of the cross-country road, were temporary dwellings made out of all sorts of material. In most of them, empty ammunition boxes played an important part. As a matter of fact, it would scarcely have been possible to carry on without them. They made excellent walls for shanties, the roof of which consisted of a tarpaulin or sail cover, secured by lacing it to wooden spares. The inside of the boxes were useful as safe places in which to keep papers and small parcels of stores which were liable to get lost.
>
> My 'dump' was just off the road, on a clean piece of turf … I eventually became possessed of three 'bell' tents with wooden 'floors', two marquees, and one or two buildings of sorts made out of packing cases and sail-covers. The telephone was installed by the R.E., and, through the Divisional Exchange, it was possible to speak with the outside world.

Omond tells of the railheads, bearing English names such as Edgehill and Grove Town, being busy places of sidings and goods yards, but also having piles of discarded stores including revolvers, field glasses, Very pistols and compasses. There were RE stores for repairing railways and roads. Ammunition dumps were 'both large and plentiful and there was need of it'. Beside the live ammunition there were piles of spent cartridge cases en route for reuse in English shell factories. The nearer to the front he got, the greater the congestion he witnessed.

Another view of railheads appeared, later, in the *RAOC Gazette* of May 1920.

It is in Flanders, in a famous and terrible salient. My office is an old shed that a Surrey cow would see the County Council about. It once had windows with glass. But shells bursting outside have long since removed the glass, and in Flanders, when glass goes, it is never replaced. Sometimes an old board, sometimes an old piece of cloth takes its place, and day by day grows more tattered, another piece of ugly-ness added to an ugly world – unutterably ugly. In the salient, spring does not bring the daffodils, nor in the summer do the trees spread their beauty in the sun.

So I sit in my dark, draughty shed, as the guns belch death to love and beauty, surrounded by a mud which, like the darkness of hell, can be felt. Pitiless rain pours down.[22]

For Omond, one moment of excitement was to see the top secret tanks 'waddling about on a firm piece of grassy land, near a railway, in the presence of HRH Prince of Wales'. These would go into action on the Somme on 15 September 1916, as explored more in the following chapter.

One of Omond's enduring memories was the noise from the constant firing of the heavy howitzers, but this would be far surpassed.

At no great distance were big guns, unseen and obstreperous, which made life wearisome with their endless noisiness. There was one gun in particular firing every ten minutes, which sent forth a projectile, which, rushing through the air at many feet per second, really sounded like an express train running through a station.

The stream of men moving to, and from the front was interminable; those going up still clean, grim but cheerful; those returning dirty and too tired, too harassed in spirits to be anything but thankful that they had escaped with their lives.

The attack made by the Division was successful, but at a cost so great, that it had to be taken out of battle at once, and sent back to rest billets to refit, leaving behind, on that blood-stained ground, some of the bravest and best of its officers and men.

Omond's first posting in France had been in a coal-mining area. The Somme was different, more like remote rural England. The trenches too were different and much inclined to filling with water. Trench foot became a major enemy. Duckboards were meant to help; more welcome

British infantry follow a Mk I into battle in September 1916. (Richard Pullen)

was the change of socks that would be brought up with the ration carts each evening. The local convent had steam-driven wringers that enabled this constant circulation.

Technology to combat gas had been developed further and Omond could issue box respirators generally rather than reserving them for machine gunners.

The division settled down for the winter witD the building of huts, incinerators, latrines, store houses, roads and rail lines. The water supply was increased. Alternative gun pits were dug.

Omond and the Deputy Assistant Quartermaster General paid a visit to the Calais Ordnance base. They were shown round the vast hangars and watched ships being unloaded as they were on a daily basis with a vast assortment of stores. They lunched well at a nearby chateau and, in the afternoon, visited the receipts depot and workshops.

The receipts depot took stores returned from the front and they were sorted by 'many French women' for cleaning and repair.

There was also an enormous hoard of scrap metal to be shipped back to England to be melted down and reused.

One particular item in the workshop caught Omond's attention: 18-pounder and 4.5in ammunition carriers. The Somme ground was too wet and soft for lorries and so pack animals had to be used. The carriers, which held eight or four of the respective rounds, helped address this. Elsewhere 'battered oilcans were being made into braziers for use in the trenches in the winter, and odd broken bits of wood into tent pegs'. Alongside workshops for saddlery, there were boot repair shops, special machinery for cleaning equipment of all sorts, a tent-menders' shop, and the armourers' and carpenters' shops.

Following Omond's experience on the Somme, he was posted as DADOS British Mission to the Portuguese Division.

> It was perhaps colder than it had been throughout a cold winter, and it must have been a very trying experience for people, many of whom had never seen snow nor frost before, to live in such a climate. The streets were thick with frozen slush and snow, and round all the street pumps were sheets of ice and long icicles. On one occasion about this time, snow fell continuously for seventy-two hours, and it was said that soldiers died from exposure in their tents.

Salvage. (RLC Archive)

Tent repairs. (RLC Archive)

Daimlers used for troop transport 1916. (Richard Pullen)

Portuguese troops arrived by train at 1.00 a.m. having eaten nothing for hours. Presented with piping hot bully beef, they spat it out and demanded coffee, which eventually was found. There is little doubt from Omond's account that there were challenges to say the least in dovetailing a foreign army into the midst of the British Army. He cites difficulties with 'training, administrative principles, discipline, languages, equipment and numerous other points'. He concludes, 'The remarkable thing is that nothing went worse than it did for, on the whole, looking back after the lapse of a certain amount of time, things really worked wonderfully well.'

AMMUNITION

In February 1918, Omond and a number of other DADOS were sent to No. 14 Ordnance Depot to learn 'what they could in ten days about ammunition'. The depot was in Flanders near the village of Zeneghem, close to what he refers to as 'the well-known depot of Audricques [*sic*]'. Alongside the ammunition depot was a transport depot and many members of the Chinese Labour Corps, who 'delighted in finding detonators in the "empties" dump out of which they would make cigarette holders'. Omond also found a 'great deal of gardening activity'. It was believed that the Canadian Corps had 80 acres of farm land. Some units kept pigs and poultry and one division was said to have a cow.

The ammunition depot itself was vast, holding 50,000 tons, but allowing a good deal of space between each ammunition sub-dump so as to reduce the risk of a major explosion. Once again he saw heaps of 'empties' destined for reuse in home shell factories. The lectures were 'most interesting', covering subjects ranging from fuses and shells, through trench mortar bombs and ending with German ammunition and fuses.

This depot was a part of the new arrangements for ammunition put into place following the devastating explosion of 20–21 July 1916. The new arrangements meant that different kinds of ammunition having different inherent risk were stored separately at least a quarter of a mile from their neighbour: boxed ammunition, component ammunition, trench munition and chemical munition. The design of depots was altered to include fire protection. The numbers of depots and ports were increased

Ammunition dump, France 1917. (RLC Archive)

and the line of communication for ammunition was formalised with Colonel Bainbridge in the North and Colonel Oldfield in the South – Tweedledum and Tweedledee, to give them their nicknames. Oldfield provided Forbes with much of the material needed for his account of the ammunition supply.

The much more elaborate systems were necessitated not only by the increased awareness of risk but also by the fast-increasing variety of ammunition being handled. Further arrangements were made to increase the facilities for technical examination and repair of ammunition by ordnance experts. Oddly, with the increase in ammunition being held, responsibility for stock at the front had passed to non-specialists until it became apparent how lackadaisical there were being. Ordnance specialists were again handed the responsibility, to the relief of all concerned. The course that Omond attended was part of this new process.

Omond was posted to Army Headquarters just before the German spring offensive in 1918.

Ordnance in all its guises had settled into the harsh rhythm of trench warfare. Better ways of doing things were found; new weapons were developed and employed; the killing power of ammunition grew and grew. The tank and increasing numbers of other motorised vehicles hinted at the potential for a more mobile war.

6

VEHICLES AND THE TANK

I n 1939 the roads of Britain were well used to all kinds of motor vehicles, from lorries and buses to motor bikes and saloon cars. Wind back just a quarter of century and the world was quite different. Of course, there were motor vehicles on the roads, but nowhere near as many. Private cars were largely the preserve of the wealthy, although Ford and some British manufacturers were making some cars for what would become the mass market. The term 'vehicle' more often described that drawn by a horse; the term 'engine' that driven by steam. Richard Pullen, in his book on the birth of the tank, records that at the start of the war the British Army had only 254 motor vehicles including lorries, cars and motor cycles.[1]

The experience of war demanded rapid change. Dewar recalled a first visit to a war zone in France in the summer of 1916:

I drove from Boulogne to Amiens one day, and for the first time fully understood that the war was being fought on wheels. Hour after hour as I left the coast, and later as I neared the Front, I passed motor transport of every description, often long lines of them almost as near one another as the carriages of a train.[2]

For someone whose book on the Second World War was entitled *War on Wheels*, I might, with great respect, take slight issue and point out that a good many of the wheels used in the Great War were either wooden for use with carts and limbers or iron to run on rails. Nevertheless, something of enormous proportions had taken place within the British motor industry to arrive at the situation that Dewar described.

Omand, from his experience as a DADOS in France, adds further evidence of the profusion of motor vehicles when he writes:

> Alongside almost every main road in the British area were parked numerous lorries of every make, and of every conceivable size. [Each lorry] was kept most beautifully clean, and the engines highly polished. Woe betide the unlucky man in charge of a lorry if his vehicle was dirty through any avoidable cause.[3]

James McMillan, writing on the story of Dunlop,[4] quite naturally points to development in rubber technology, such as the pneumatic tyre, as certainly a good part of the reason why the motor vehicle moved closer to centre stage. The writers of the history of the Wolseley Motor Company[5] are unequivocal that it was the development of the internal combustion engine itself.

> For the first time in history of warfare the internal combustion engine was employed in 1914 on the high seas, in the air and on land by both sides, and the more it was employed, all the greater became its possibilities.[6]

Earlier they had pointed out rather prosaically that:

> Steadily the Metallurgist, the Scientist and the Engineer began to rank in importance with the General in the field; the older and perhaps more chivalrous type of conflict of the Napoleonic days was passing, just as the bow and arrow of the sixteenth century had to give place to the firearm.

In his history of the Albion Motor Company, *Sure as the Sunrise*, Sam McKinstry offers a helpful overview of the British motor industry at the outbreak of the First World War. He suggests that it was employing 100,000 people, adding that Daimler alone had 5,000 workers, Wolseley 4,000, Sunbeam and Humber perhaps 3,000. In 1913 those companies produced 1,000, 3,000, 2,500 and 1,700 chassis respectively.[7]

A 3-tonner. (RLC Archive)

THE SUBSIDY SCHEME AND IMPRESSMENT

In the summer of 1914, with the coming of war, the Wolseley authors tell how the greatest need as expressed by the War Office was for staff cars, ambulances and lorries. Accordingly, requisitions were made of all such vehicles at the factory awaiting delivery, all such vehicles held by distributors and those vehicles that had recently been delivered to customers.

The story at Leyland[8] was not dissimilar, again from August 1914:

> Another observer who was in the heart of London at that time had recorded that the only event that he personally remembered clearly was the assembling in London, from all quarters of Great Britain, of Waring and Gillow's fine fleet of subsidy lorries, their hasty stripping, in the pouring rain, of civilian trimmings and their equally hasty fitting with accessories of war.

McKinstry is also helpful in unravelling the subsidy scheme. Its origin was with horses where, in return for an annual retainer, the government could in time of war requisition the horses it would need. The experience of the Boer War had shown the tragedy of some 500,000 horses dying in army service and so the horse scheme was adapted for

Some 3-tonners gathering. (RLC Archive)

use with motorised vehicles. The 1911 scheme provided an initial subsidy of between £8 and £12 per vehicle, giving the military the option
to buy them at written-down value plus 25 per cent. Vehicles had to
meet the War Office specification and had to be inspected annually. As
with horses, the purpose of the scheme was to have sufficient vehicles at
the government's disposal without the need to maintain and store large
numbers.[9] In the years up to the start of the First World War, this scheme
underwent further revisions.

It soon became clear, though, that there were insufficient 'subsidy'
vehicles for the 'Contemptible Little Army' and so army impressment
officers were sent out with a list of other suitable vehicles that would
then be pressed into service. The companies themselves were forbidden
to provide vehicles for civilian use and had instead to concentrate their
production on vehicles of the 'subsidy' types.

> At Leyland itself the force of authority was very soon felt. Army officers
> swooped down on the factory and stopped all civilian deliveries. Buses,
> covered vans, platform lorries and all other kinds of vehicles passing
> through its shops were hurriedly stripped of their body work and speedily-
> built high-sided WD [War Department] pattern bodywork substituted.[10]

The war presented the fledgling motor industry with a massive challenge.

THE MOTOR COMPANIES

Albion was proudly Scottish. It had been created by two engineers, Thomas Murray and Norman Fulton, and began business at the turn of the twentieth century on the edge of the docklands of the upper Clyde. By 1903 it had expanded and moved into new premises. The situation, though, was dire; British industry, once supreme, was now a laggard.

'In March 1903, William Weir, addressing the Royal Scottish Automobile Club, noted that while about 2,500 cars a year were being built in Britain, about 3,500 were imported.'[11]

Albion prepared to take up the challenge. By dint of inventive engineering and enthusiastic marketing, by 1912 the company was producing nearly 500 chassis a year. These were mainly commercials, reflecting the predominant use being made of motor vehicles as delivery vans. In 1913 the company expanded into a new factory block built with the new technology of ferro-concrete as used, for example, by Ford in the USA.

On the declaration of war, Albion, like the other British motor companies, had its stock of A10 32hp vehicles requisitioned and all future production impressed. With the likelihood of further demands, the directors decided on an expansion of their new factory.

There were, though, problems ahead. There simply were not enough skilled male engineers to meet the demands of production and those there were resisted the employment of lesser skilled workers. Albion thus shared in the industrial unrest that hit Beardmore and other Clyde engineers, but as with them, the Dilution scheme was eventually accepted and able men were released to the colours and women introduced to the workforce.

Production of War Office vehicles increased each year from 591 in 1914 to 1,843 in 1918, giving a total wartime production of 5,594.[12] McKinstry reports that the company received an official commendation to the effect that Albion vehicles 'were head and shoulders above all other makes ... [a big factor] in obtaining such happy results being, in the opinion of the War Office, the Murray-Albion system of lubrication.' It was a time of technical innovation and successful ideas made a difference.

In contrast to Albion, Foden, which would go on to produce heavy internal combustion engine vehicles for the army in the Second World War, in the First World War remained largely dedicated to steam. Once again, at the start of hostilities, the War Office requisitioned some 100 Foden wagons. These could not be used near the front, where the steam and glow from the firebox would offer an easy target to artillery, but they undertook vital heavy work behind the lines.[13]

Daimler had its origins in Germany in the 1880s. In 1896, Harry Lawson, a wealthy Coventry man already manufacturing cycles, purchased the Daimler patents and formed the Daimler Motor Company Limited. Alan Townsin explains that the early years were, as for many entrepreneurial businesses, both challenging (the company folded and re-emerged as the Daimler Motor Company in 1904) and inventive, and great advances were made particularly with the manufacture of buses. Importantly, the talented engineer William Lanchester joined the company. In 1910, BSA acquired Daimler and Frank Searle, chief engineer of the London General Omnibus Company, joined to set up a new commercial department. With the 105hp sleeve valve engine at

Daimler 30cwt WD lorry. (Copyright Jaguar Daimler Heritage Trust)

Daimler Coventry Motor Mills factory c.1909. (Copyright Jaguar Daimler Heritage Trust)

Daimler WD lorries. (Copyright Jaguar Daimler Heritage Trust)

its heart, Daimler under Searle produced a 3-ton lorry to War Office specification. The familiar requisitioning of stock and impressment of future production occurred[14] and Daimler joined in the war effort.

The 105hp engine was to go on to power heavy duty track-laying tractors in conjunction with Fosters of Lincoln, and also the first tank. Frank Searle would go on to serve with distinction in the Tank Corps. Daimler would also produce staff cars, and ambulances. The Daimler engine was used in the AEC truck chassis for War Office work.[15]

AEC was another example of the intricate web of the motor industry. The Associated Equipment Co. Ltd had been registered on 13 June 1912 and took over the already busy bus chassis manufacturing business from its then owner, the London General Omnibus Company Ltd.[16] In 1914 LGOC suffered the same fate as other vehicle manufacturers and opera-tors when 1,185 of its buses were pressed into use and soon could be seen transporting troops in France and Belgium.[17] AEC began producing on its own account in June 1916 and by the end of the war had supplied 5,200 heavy-duty 3-ton vehicles using the Tyler engine.[18]

Thornycroft began production in the mid-nineteenth century, but with boats rather than land-based vehicles. The Thornycroft steam vehicle was developed by the founder's son, whose company was incorporated into the shipbuilding company in the early twentieth century. Thornycroft developed a petrol-driven vehicle and joined the subsidy scheme, its J-type lorry becoming the most popular in the First World War. This particular type found other uses, including having an anti-aircraft gun mounted on its back.[19] Some 5,000 vehicles were supplied to the army in the First World War.

The Humber Company offers further strands of the web. Tom Humber began work as an engineer in Nottingham and set up the first Humber factory at Beeston, from which the Chilwell explosion of 1 July 1918 would have been clearly heard. Humber began with bicycles, moved on to motor cycles and then produced motor cars, famously the 1903 single-cylinder Humberette, both from Beeston and from a new factory in Coventry. In the first decade of the twentieth century and in the second, Humber boasted a range of engine sizes and body types.

The coming of war did 'not immediately bring car production to a halt and full catalogue was produced for 1915'.[20] With the general move away from civilian production, 'warlike' options were produced in the form of delivery vans using the 10hp and 11hp engines and ambulances with the larger 14hp. Bentley had a particular contribution to the war effort in the shape of the aluminium piston invented by W.O. Bentley.[21] Humber produced aero engines to his design. Humber also manufactured 'the sort of war materials that could equally well be done by a much smaller, less well-equipped and less experienced concern'.[22]

Commercial Cars Limited produced field workshop vehicles for the Red Cross to maintain ambulances. In 1926, the Humber Motor Company took control of the company and changed its name to Commer Cars Limited.[23] Karrier, another of the companies, which with Humber and Commer would become the Rootes Group, produced a ¾-tonner that was accepted under the subsidy scheme and some 3,000 were produced for the services. The Vulcan Motor Company produced some 100 chassis a week for the War Office during the First World War from its factory at Southport. Vulcan production was eventually taken over by Tilling Stevens at Maidstone, whose factory also became part of the Rootes Group in 1952.[24]

The Sunbeam Motor Company, subsequently another Rootes Company, had its origins in bicycles. Its founder, John Marsden, appointed a Frenchman, Louis Coatalen, chief engineer in 1909 and he designed car engines and also engines for First World War aeroplanes. An early Sunbeam was reputedly the first car ever to be driven at more than 200mph.[25]

The Wolseley Company had begun as a manufacturer of sheep-shearing machinery in Australia. Herbert Austin became involved after he had spent a highly constructive 'apprenticeship' with a number of engineering companies around Melbourne, to where his uncle had persuaded him to move.

The head office of the firm moved to London in 1890 and Austin developed further the machine technology, also branching out into machine tools and parts for cycles. It was probably in about 1895 that the first 'Austin' car appeared branded, of course, Wolseley. Austin was clearly a great innovator but, it was said, was held back by the other Wolseley directors.

Towards the end of the century Vickers and Sir Hiram Maxim were exploring the possibilities of motor car-related inventions and made an investment in Wolseley. In 1901 Vickers registered as a subsidiary, the Wolseley Tool and Motor Car Company Ltd, and moved production to the Adderley Park Works in Birmingham with factory floor space covering 17 acres. Roy Church suggests that Austin's commitment to his side valve engine held the company back, with the result that Austin left in

1905 to pursue his own business. Austin's departure coincided with the arrival of rival engineer J.D. Siddeley but it seems with no immediate greater commercial success.[26]

Under Vickers' ownership, as well as wheeled vehicles Wolseley would contribute to the war effort by developing and producing aero engines, most notably the Viper, some 3 million shells and also firing gear and gunsights for the Royal Navy.[27] The writer of the *Diary of an Old Contemptible* talks of his Wolseley pattern helmet, which performed the duties of an egg basket in Mesopotamia when they sought out supplements to an inadequate diet.[28]

Herbert Austin set up the Austin Motor Company in 1905 in a former print works at Longbridge near Birmingham. During the war the company would go on to produce 8 million shells, 650 guns, 2,000 aeroplanes, 500 armoured cars and other equipment such as generating sets, pumping equipment, aeroplane engines, ambulances and lorries.[29]

The firm of White & Poppe in Coventry offers another link in the spider's web of firms engaged in war production. W.R.M. Motors, run by W.R. Morris, who would later become Lord Nuffield, began production of the Morris-Oxford in 1914. Its engine, gearbox and clutch were made by White & Poppe, and Morris developed a strong working relationship, particularly with Mr Poppe. Morris, though, had the ambition to produce a car that could compete with Ford on price. He therefore explored the USA for component suppliers and found that Continental Motors could produce an engine for half of what he paid White & Poppe. This was for the Morris-Cowley and Morris placed orders for 1,500 engines just as war was breaking out.

Morris had acquired premises in Cowley and had built a steel extension, giving him a large area in which to assemble cars. Unfortunately, for Morris, the war meant that demand for such vehicles would be strictly limited and so, over the war years, he made only 1,300 yet still honouring his US contract. This placed him in a precarious position and he sought War Office work. He was first awarded a contract for Stokes mortar bomb cases. The success of this led him to be asked to manufacture mine sinkers. Here the space he had available came into its own and he assembled these devices from parts supplied, but in large numbers, reaching 2,000 per week. The original supplier had offered an upper limit of forty.[30]

MOTOR CYCLES

The motor cycle certainly ranked higher than the lorry in numerical terms. Its use by the army was principally by despatch riders, but there were others. My own father, Bill Williams, had volunteered for the Machine Gun Corps because officers were issued with motor cycles. He parted company with his when he and the cycle met a wall at speed. He then transferred to the Army Ordnance Corps, attracted by bomb disposal.[31] In his book on the Douglas Motor Cycle, J.R. Clew observed, writing about the Douglas 2¾hp twin, that 'it had a charm all of its own, was very sweet running and would respond well to the tuning that some of the more competent artificers were able to give'.[32]

The Douglas Company was founded in Bristol in the latter part of the nineteenth century as a boot machine repairer. It progressed into foundry work and in the first decade of the twentieth century made first forays into motor cycles. The design skill came from Joseph Barter who had developed a small machine known as the Fairy. Willie Douglas and Barter were true motor cycle enthusiasts participating in the early years of motor sport. The breakthrough came in 1910 and by the start of the war they had produced some 12,000 machines. During the First World War they manufactured 25,000 motor cycles for army use.[33]

Douglas motorcycle. (RLC Archive)

Clew adds flesh to the bones of the bare facts about Douglas when he describes the experience of Gerald Young, who served through the war years as a despatch rider. Young served in the trenches for nine months, with his Douglas 'kept in a hut reserved for the more seriously wounded'.[34] He then moved back to headquarters at Abbeville. 'He experienced the odd drop into an unexpected shell hole, like most of his fellow riders, but had far less trouble with tyres and tubes than expected, even though he frequently took to the rough.' The reference to inner tubes is probably a reference to the practice riders had of dispensing with the heavy spare parts box, and instead carrying the necessary spares on their person, 'wearing the inner tube as a collar to save it from damage'.

Triumph had its origins in the bicycle boom of the 1880s. It was founded by another German, Siegfried Bettmann, as a wholesale business of bicycles manufactured in Birmingham. It prospered and began manufacturing in its own premises in Coventry. It was there that it attracted the attention of Harvey du Cros, who had provided financial backing for John Boyd Dunlop, and the Dunlop company made an investment in Triumph.[35] The manufacture of a motor cycle began in 1902. The outbreak of war brought another name into the Triumph equation: Claude V. Holbrook, a staff captain with the purchasing branch of the War Office. The authors recount how:

Five despatch riders and their Triumph motorcycles take a break in 1915. (Richard Pullen)

One Sunday morning, with the war but a few weeks old, the telephone rang in Bettmann's home. Could Triumph, asked Captain Holbrook, pack and ship to France, urgently, 100 motor cycles for the British Expeditionary Force? Bettmann promised to do the best he could and set out for the home of his works manager, Charles Hathaway. In turn Hathaway rounded up as many Triumph workers as he could find, opened up the Priory Street plant, and got the job under way.[36]

Triumph supplied some 30,000 motor cycles during the First World War. These were virtually all the model H, 'the 550cc side valve, with chain primary drive, a Sturmey-Archer three-speed gearbox incorporating a clutch and kick starter and a belt final drive'. They were nicknamed the Trusty but by all accounts 'the army boys liked the model H'.

THE MAGNETO

Very soon into the war a potentially fatal stumbling block was encountered. The War Department vehicle specification stipulated the Bosch magneto – clearly, with the German company very much on the opposing side, this was no longer sensible. Worse than that though, Bosch had a UK market share of some 90 per cent. For a number of reasons, UK manufacturers simply did not make magnetos nor many of their component parts that Dewar lists: varnished silk, cambric and paper, ruby mica, tinfoil, aluminium and copper die castings, insulating baking varnish, Egyptian cotton take, silk tubes of fine bore, ball bearings, carbon brushings, ebonite rod and sheet.

There was though one company, Thomson-Bennett of Birmingham, which in 1914 was turning out twenty-five magnetos a week. Slowly this company's production increased and other companies were drawn by the Ministry into magneto production. Much the same was true of spark plugs – British companies were producing 5,000 a year before the war, but, by the end, production had increased to 300,000.

THE TANK

'The Germans were beaten … not by the genius of Marshal Foch but by "General Tank"'. So said German historian Gen der Infanterie A.W.H. von Zwehl.

This assertion has been much debated. George Forty[37] puts some numbers to it. 'Between September 1916 and November 1918, British tanks took part in 3,060 separate engagements, French in 4,356 and American in 250. For a book on equipping the British Army, the French figure remains significant; in no sense were they a junior partner in the Entente. Forty suggests that once the French had seen the effectiveness of the Holt tractor towing artillery guns, they pressed ahead with Schneider and St Chamond heavy tanks as well as the Renault FT-17 light tanks series. I explore in Chapter 8 the Holt tractor and later in this chapter the relationship of French tank production to that of the British.

This, though, is a book on the equipping of the British Army and so it is mainly to British manufacturers that I now turn my attention. Not, though, immediately to the tank, for in 1914 that was only an idea; at that stage no one had worked out how one might actually be built or operated. For 1914 the down-to-earth reality of armoured warfare was the Royal Navy Armoured Car Division.

The British Royal Naval Air Service (RNAS), Livesey[38] suggests, encountered armoured vehicles being used effectively by the Belgian Army in 1914. These armoured vehicles were in truth touring cars armed with boiler plate and equipped with one or more machine guns. The RNAS developed a small number of tourers for use in rescuing downed aircraft and it armed a couple of these, finding them of use against German cavalry.

Given the effectiveness of this improvised weapon, the Royal Navy Armoured Car Division (RNACD) was formed in October 1914 with fifteen armoured squadrons. The design eventually standardised on the Rolls-Royce chassis. George Oliver notes with obvious pride that 'within their limits Rolls-Royce armoured cars were most effective fighting vehicles – absolutely dependable, fast and manoeuvrable'.[39] The use of armoured cars on the Western Front, though, was short-lived given that the mobile phase of the war gave way to static trench warfare where armoured vehicles in any numbers would be of comparatively little use.

Rolls-Royce armoured car converted from a Silver Ghost. (Copyright Rolls-Royce Plc)

Armoured car. (Copyright Rolls-Royce Plc)

Attempts were made to use armoured cars in Gallipoli, but without success. More fruitful ground was found in Egypt, where the army 'reluctantly took charge of them and used them for patrolling the Suez Canal'. They came into their own in desert operations, not as a strategic weapon, but rather when used imaginatively by individual officers. Famously, Lawrence of Arabia made good use of a Rolls-Royce armoured car.

There remained the massive and inescapable tragedy that young British men were being slaughtered in their thousands because no one had yet come up with an effective defence against machine guns. It was five months since Haig had told the British War Council: 'The machine gun is a much overrated weapon and two per battalion more than sufficient.' Gilbert suggests that he was once again proved terribly wrong, as evidenced by this German regimental account from Loos in September 1915:

> The men stood on the fire-steps, some even on parapets, and fired triumphantly into the mass of men advancing across open grassland. As the entire field of fire was covered with the enemy's infantry, the effect was devastating and they could be seen falling literally in hundreds.[40]

This horrific situation was well known to the powers that be. Gilbert records that Churchill had written to Prime Minister Asquith suggesting that a number of steam tractors could be protected by armour plate and used to transport soldiers in safety under fire. If used at night the steam would not be seen and the use of caterpillar tracks would enable the crossing of trenches.[41]

In his book *The Dunlop Story*, James McMillan tells how Winston Churchill, as First Lord of the Admiralty, asked Admiral Bacon, the general manager of the Coventry Ordnance Works, to draw up plans for a 'landship' capable of crossing trenches.[42] When tested in May 1915 the resulting vehicle failed its trials. Nevertheless, Churchill was not to be put off and sanctioned Sir Eustace Tennyson-d'Encourt, the chief constructor of the navy, to take charge of the landship project. A Landships Committee was formed with Albert Steer as secretary.

This was crucial but it was far from a standing start. H.G. Wells had written about landships, but there were more concrete examples.

Armament Staff Sergeant L.S. Jeffcoate did not leave a diary, but rather a box full of photographs and mementoes. From this it is possible to gather that he was a skilled technician. He began in the Royal

Armament Sgt L.S. Jeffcoate.
(RLC Archive)

Engineers and was involved in
experimental wireless in 1905.
In 1906 he received a second-
class certificate of education
and was based at Chatham
as an instrument repairer. In
December 1917 he was in No. 8
Ordnance Mobile workshop
attached to the Canadian Corps
Troops Supply Column. In June
1915 he must have served at Le
Havre because he had a leave
pass on 1 June, on the reverse of
which there is a long list of cafes
placed out of bounds.[43]

In the box there is a photograph dated 1907 of a oil-powered tractor with caterpillar tracks. It was probably made by Richard Hornsby
& Sons. It does however provide a starting point since two of the three
essential features are present: caterpillar tracks and armour plating. All that
is missing is the gun or guns.

Lincoln-based military historian Richard Pullen has, in his book
The Landships of Lincoln, researched just how the tank moved from being
an idea tobecome a machine that could be deployed in battle. Others
too have explored the subject. All are agreed that two men in particular
should take credit for the tank's design.

Walter Wilson was an engineer who had designed an armoured car
and gun tractor for Armstrong Whitworth in 1906. It had been, it seems,
rather ahead of its time and Wilson then worked as a freelance engineer until he joined the Royal Navy Armoured Car Service in 1914.
He became involved with the Admiralty Landships Committee and in
1915 he was seconded to small Lincoln-based engineering company,
William Foster and Co. Ltd.[44]

Fosters was owned and managed by another gifted engineer, William
Tritton. Fosters was far too small a company either to produce entire

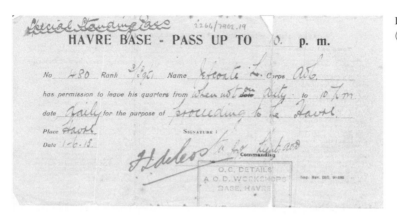

Le Havre pass.
(RLC Archive)

Out of bounds.
(RLC Archive)

First tractor in
the British Army,
Aldershot 1907.
(RLC Archive)

Some of the employees of William Foster and Co. in 1917. (Richard Pullen)

tanks or to assemble all the tanks that the army would eventually demand. However, it did have the remarkable skills of these two men plus a gifted draftsman, William Rigby, and a skilled and loyal workforce. It was based in a city steeped in engineering. In time the male workforce was more than ably supported by an influx of women, like so many others across the land leaning their shoulders to the war effort.

It wasn't, though, always to be Fosters. J.R. Hume, in his account of Beardmore's contribution to the war effort, makes the point, as almost an aside, that Armstrong Whitworth had been asked to develop the tank but had declined. This story is expanded upon a little in Scott's history of Vickers. Here Colonel Swinton, one of the champions of the tank at the War Office, is said to have met Admiral Ottley of Armstrongs in Pall Mall and told him the whole story, offering to supply the drawings if Armstrongs would take up the development of the tank as a private venture. The admiral was sympathetic, but Swinton heard no more about it.[45]

I may be wrong in reading any significance into this, but in many ways it does make sense. From the start, the tank did not have that many fans. The Landships Committee and Colonel Albert Stern, and indeed

Swinton, were very much in favour. However, the army needed guns and Armstrongs made them. They were thus biased in favour of what they were already doing to great effect. The same was not the case with Fosters. It was not then even a recognised War Office manufacturer; its employees were not regarded as being in reserved occupations. It was thus much better placed to undertake what was an uncertain project and Wilson and Tritton set to work.

The starting point was in a sense the town of Grantham, south of Lincoln, where the engineering company, Richard Hornsby & Sons, had developed an agricultural tractor with caterpillar tracks. Radically, this tractor was powered by an oil engine instead of the more conventional steam.[46] The tractor was not a commercial success and Hornsby sold the patents to the Holt Tractor Company of Stockton, California, as Holts were in a far better position to develop the technology. Lincolnshire, though, remained in the picture with Ruston and Proctor Ltd manufacturing 75bhp tractors, under licence from Holts, for the British Army.

Ruston and Proctor Ltd had been engineers in Lincoln since the mid-nineteenth century. Their core business was steam-driven diggers or navvies as they were nicknamed. Ruston Steam Navvys famously dug the Manchester Ship Canal. During the war the Rustons factory did indeed produce 440 caterpillar tractors along with armaments ranging from wagons of all types to wheels, gun mountings, horseshoes, shells and bombs,

Gun tractor. (RLC Archive)

tank trailers, engines and sponsons as well as aircraft. Rustons manufactured 2,750 aircraft, 3,200 engines and complete spares for a further 800 aircraft.[47] In September 1918 Ruston would join with Hornsby, whose oil engine had also aided the war effort and which set it on course for a bright future.

The next stage in development of the tank was with Tritton, who had been asked by the Admiralty to design and produce a tractor capable of towing a 15in howitzer. The Tritton Silent Knight with a Daimler 105hp engine fitted the bill. It did, however, have to stop when it came to a trench and soldiers had to get out in order to lay a suitable bridge. From this came the Tritton Trench Crosser, which sadly never made it into production, but it had taught Wilson and Tritton enough for them to begin the design of the Number 1 Lincoln Machine.

Pullen points to one further piece of the jigsaw. The Holt caterpillar tracks had not been entirely successful and another American track manufacturer came into play with the Bullock Creeping Grip California Giant Tractor. Developing the track technology from the ideas in both, Wilson and Tritton developed a tracked machine that became 'Little Willie'. It never went into action but became the template from which tanks would develop.

Charles Maughan is a name absent from the other accounts of the tank's story, but Richard Pullen draws in this Lincoln man who was chief tester and engineer for Fosters because he was the first man ever to drive a tank. Pullen offers a further anecdote. Little Willie was put through its paces in Hatfield Park in the presence of the King. It seems that a young naval lieutenant had been allocated to Maughan as gearsman for the day. The story goes that the gearsman made such a mess of his duties that Maughan tore him off a good number of strips, only to remember that behind them in the tank sat His Majesty. Maughan looked round, fearing the Tower of London or worse, only to find the King highly amused. Maughan immediately took advantage of this good humour and obtained the King's autograph: something quite unheard of.[48]

A.J. Smithers, in his book, *Cambrai The First Tank Battle*, tells how almost as Little Willie was being demonstrated a wooden mock-up of a 'lozenge-shaped contraption' was taken by Stern to the Trench Warfare Experimental Ground at Wembley. This revised design overcame the shortcoming of Little Willie's tracks.

The tracking used on Little Willie had proved problematic and Wilson and Tritton came up with the idea that the tracks should not run on

One of the best photographs of a Great War tank, Mother during her trials at Burton Park in January 1916. (Richard Pullen)

bogies under the tanks but rather should travel all around the hull. With these, trenches could be crossed and barbed wire trampled.

The tracks on which the tank would run were driven by rubber wheels along the base of the track and solid-tyred idler wheels where the track wound around the top of the tank. Dunlop had to develop rubber that could withstand the sort of temperatures that were generated by the tank tracks.[49]

Dunlop at that time was run by the du Cross family under its patriarch Harvey du Cross, known as the Napoleon of the tyre industry, and in 1916 built its iconic factory, Fort Dunlop, in Birmingham. The work on making a rubber that could withstand high temperatures led to the development of the pneumatic tyre and so to the massive contribution Dunlop made in the Second World War.[50] Sir Eric Geddes who, with his statistician partner George Beharrell, made such a massive contribution principally to transport in the First World War, would go on, with their sons Reay Geddes and Edward Beharrell, to 'dominate Dunlop for some fifty years'.[51]

The new tank, 'Mother', was demonstrated just as the news of the slaughter resulting from men marching into uncut wire and massed machine guns at the Battle of Loos became public knowledge.

Even then von Dunlop and others remained unconvinced. 'He viewed with dismay the fact that the War Office, the Committee of Imperial Defence and the Admiralty were all mixed up in deciding this question. He was also somewhat annoyed that he should have been asked to provide guns and ammunition when he had not been consulted as to their pattern,' Smithers adds that 'perhaps it was as well that he had been excluded, a 2.95in mountain gun was borrowed from Woolwich and proved satisfactory, but it was impossible to get, so in the end the 6-pounder naval gun was adopted'.[52]

The Secretary of State for War Lord Kitchener, who had drowned when HMS *Hampshire*, which was taking him to a conference in Russia, sank when torpedoed off Orkney on 6 June 1916, had never shared the enthusiasm of some of his colleagues for the tank, which he saw from the start as being vulnerable to enemy artillery. The cavalry didn't like it because it still believed that the horse remained supreme in mobile warfare. Also, as became apparent in the desert, non-tank officers simply did not know how to use them effectively. Nevertheless, the genie was out of the bottle and the tank was here to stay.

The development of the tank thus proceeded with 'Mother'. This larger beast had the same Daimler-Foster 105hp engine, chassis and gearbox and was armed with two Vickers water-cooled machine guns and 6-pounder guns made by Armstrongs.

Pullen has another story of when Mother was put through her paces in Burton Park just outside Lincoln. Thomas Hetherington and Albert Stern thought it was about time really to test her by firing the 6-pounders. Hetherington took aim and squeezed the trigger. Silence. Then without warning the gun fired and no trace of the shell could be found. The sight of Lincoln Cathedral within easy range must surely have made the blood drain from the faces of the two men. Happily, with time and a good deal of digging the shell was discovered buried in the parkland. To round off a good story, it is said that Hetherington had bet Wilson that the tank would fall apart when the gun was fired. It didn't and Mother became the blueprint for the Mk 1 Tank, which went into action on 15 September 1916.

That first tank action comprised forty-nine machines, of which only thirty-two managed to get to the starting line and, of these, ten were put out of action by artillery.[53] This experience provoked a variety of responses. Churchill was despondent that his idea had been used too early and on too small a scale. The French were angry that the secret of

Mother at Burton Park in early 1916. (Richard Pullen)

Beardmore tank. (University of Glasgow Archives & Special Collections, William Beardmore & Co. Ltd collection, GB 0248 UGD 100/1/11/3/page 66)

the tank had been let out for so little gain. In time, though, many saw the benefit of the experience as a test of the tank in battle from which they could learn. Gilbert suggests that 'recognising the potential of the weapon, Haig asked the War Office for a thousand of them'.[54]

The tanks that appeared on the Somme were all to Tritton and Wilson's design but Fosters did not have the capacity to manufacture all of them and so most were made by the Metropolitan Carriage, Wagon and Finance Company of Birmingham.[55]

Haig's demand for a thousand was, though, altogether on a different scale and so four more firms were enlisted into tank production: Armstrong Whitworth, the Coventry Ordnance Works, Beardmore, and Mirrless Watson & Co. of Glasgow.[56]

All the time, though, Tritton and Wilson were working at overcoming the faults that came to light when tanks went into action. A Mk II and a Mk III were produced, but without armour and intended for use only in training. Significantly, the Vickers machine guns were replaced by the cheaper Lewis gun. The Lewis, although very effective when used by the infantry, did not work well in the tank, its jacket and barrel being too vulnerable to attack. Such was the shortage of armaments, though, that despite protests the Lewis was there to stay. The Mk IV, built for action, had the Lewis but mounted differently and so a little less vulnerable.

The tank was a piece of engineering and, like all such pieces, demanded both maintenance and modification.

Tanks were allocated initially to the Heavy Branch, Machine Gun Corps, possibly because of its proximity to Lincoln, based as it was in Grantham.[57] It was not until July 1917 that a separate Tank Corps was created.

At the start, in September and October 1916, armament and ammunition aspects came within the responsibilities of the DADOS, of which the formation of the tank was part. In November of that year Lieutenant Sir Edward Nightingale was appointed Ordnance officer to the Heavy Branch, Machine Gun Corps and by the end of December all tanks had been transferred to this formation. Nightingale was replaced by a permanent DADOS and workshops were set up at Tanks Corps Headquarters at Bermicourt. Not long afterwards the stores and workshops relocated to Erin, where the Central Ordnance Workshop was then based for the duration.[58]

Mk IV tanks being built at Fosters in early 1917. (Richard Pullen)

In preparation for the action at Cambrai, the Central Workshop was a hive of activity. Tanks that had previously seen action were in need of patching up. New tanks straight from the factory had to be prepared. A.J. Smithers suggests the need to look back into military history for a key piece of military equipment for the planned tank attack: fascines. These were very large bundles of wood, tied with chains and carried on the top of tanks, to be dropped into trenches to allow the tanks to drive over. Chinese labour at the workshops would prepare the bundles and then the chains would be fastened round using two tanks to pull together the ends. Some 350 such fascines were produced.[59]

Another piece of preparation concerned what were known as 'fills'. Smithers refers to the thirst of the Daimler engine. A 'fill' consisted of '60 gallons of petrol, 10 of oil, 20 of water, 10 lbs of grease, 10,000 rounds of .303 for the females (armed only with machine guns) and 200 6-lb rounds for the male plus 6,000 small arms rounds'. The transport of these 'fills' posed a challenge. The solution was sledges made of wood in the Central Workshop that could be loaded with the 'fills' and other items and then dragged in threes behind a tank.[60]

Smithers describes the scene before Cambrai:

The great muster of the tanks, the first glimpse of what war of the future would be, was nearly complete. There were 378 fighting machines, fifty-four supply tanks with sledges, thirty-two fitted with grapnels for dragging wire out of the way of the horses, two more carrying bridging material also for use of the cavalry, nine fitted with wireless and the last carrying telephone cable for the Third Army.[61]

The Mk IV tank went into action at Cambrai in November 1917, this time with great effect. Eyewitnesses described how the tank laid bare paths for infantry to follow and how those defending trenches hardly had time to flee before the tanks were upon them.[62]

Three further developments merit particular comment.

The tank as originally conceived was difficult to steer and so when the prospect of mobile battles became a reality the Whippet was conceived with two engines, one for each track. Steering was accomplished by varying the comparative speed of the engines, a juggling act of some complexity with the driver having to grapple with two full sets of controls. In her paper, *Technology Development in Coalition: The Case of the First World War Tank*,[63] Elizabeth Greenhalgh observes that the French Renault tank was

A brand new Male Mk IV paid for by the Federal Council of the Malay States in 1917. (Richard Pullen)

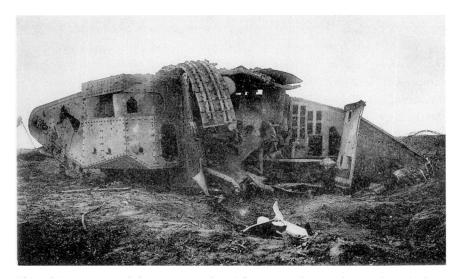

This Mk II was captured almost intact and used for tests involving stick grenades and other small explosive charges. (Richard Pullen)

This 1918 press photograph shows German guns being retrieved from the battlefield by British tanks after Cambrai. (Richard Pullen)

possibly better than the Whippet because of its greater manoeuvrability and speed but also because it could be transported by lorry. More to the point, though, she argues that the French and British could and probably should have cooperated more, with the French producing lighter tanks and the British the heavier ones but for common use. She cites incident after incident when cooperation could have been possible but was rejected.

Another development focused on the Daimler engine. The 105hp simply was not strong enough to move tons of tank over rough ground for any length of time. The solution came in the person of the talented motor engineer, Harry Ricardo. He approached the leading engine manufacturers, Daimler, Sunbeam and Rolls-Royce, and was told that they were more than willing to manufacture but had not the resources to design and test. Ricardo therefore designed a 150hp engine that went on to power the Mk V. The version was developed further and was that principally engaged in the final months of the war.

The final development followed the entry of the USA into the war and took the form of the Mk VIII, and I turn not to Pullen but to George Dewar. The Mk VIII was to be an Allied tank and in the autumn of 1918 Dewar witnessed them being made in one of the factories near Manchester.

> The plates for the hull of Mark VIII were reaching the factory when I visited it in three forms – armour plates, bomb-proof plates and mild steel. They were drilled and cut to the required dimensions, heated in furnaces, dipped red-hot into baths of whale oil for tempering, and a few minutes later drawn out to be hammered flat by hand work – heavy labour fit only for strong men. Women were working in this tank hull factory, but here was a man's exclusive department.[64]

Dewar goes on to describe the factory as being one of great order, necessary because the Mk VIII had no fewer than 730 different parts requiring some 620 templets. Whippets were also being assembled in the same factory. Dewar witnessed the engine for the Mk VIII which developed 300hp at 1,200rpm. Pullen[65] adds that the engine was a V12 derived from an aero engine. The tank was named the Liberty Tank or International.

The Mk VIII project, Greenhalgh explains, was to be a truly Entente project. She records the seemingly endless arguments over which army should receive them first. In the event the Armistice came before the first VIII was ready for action.

7

OTHER THEATRES OF WAR – PALESTINE, MESOPOTAMIA, ITALY AND RUSSIA

PALESTINE

In 1915 the task facing the British and Allied forces in Egypt had been its defence from tribesmen in the west and from the Turks in the east. The first imperative was to prevent the Turks from crossing Suez into Egypt. Second to this was the preservation of the Suez Canal for the exclusive use of the Allies. The first of these objectives was really only an extension of the existing role of the British in their protectorate. To this end, the relatively small force would be equipped from the existing peacetime ordnance establishment.

The end of Gallipoli campaign, however, saw the start of more significant activity around the Suez Canal and up into Palestine with the ambition of final victory over the Turks driving them out of both Palestine and Syria.

The starting point for ordnance, as with Gallipoli, was Alexandria, which by the end of 1915 had become an established Ordnance base.

In 1916 the volumes passing through Alexandria were large with nearly 7 million tons on some 1,200 ships.[1] Workshops had been set up, local suppliers engaged and storage facilities, covering a number of acres, put into place for all manner of stores including ammunition.

Lawrence's Arab force was supplied from Alexandria with effective use of armoured cars, which, as already mentioned, were Rolls-Royce tourers, with armour plate and a machine gun.

Some eight Mk 1 tanks saw action in Gaza in January 1917. Their effectiveness though was significantly reduced by the inability of senior officers to understand how best to employ them.[2] Sand also proved to be a problem and is an example of lessons being learnt for the Second World War, where processes of 'desertisation' were employed to great effect.

At the start of 1916, Alexandria saw very large numbers of Australian and New Zealand troops arrive and make their way along the Canal. These troops had been through the mill in Gallipoli and needed completely re-equipping. There were also freshly arrived troops, who needed kitting out for the local environment. It soon became clear that

T.E. Lawrence in a Rolls-Royce armoured car. (Copyright Rolls-Royce Plc)

AOC Camp Alexandria. (RLC Archive)

Tank after repairs at AOC Alexandria. (RLC Archive)

local depots would be needed and these were established at Port Said, Ferry Post (Ismailia), Suez and Tel el Kebir, which would re-emerge in 1940 as the key ordnance base for the Desert War.

Brigadier General Bainbridge, who wrote the 'official' Army Ordnance account of the Palestine Campaign, was appointed DOS Palestine,[3] having returned from Gallipoli via Alexandria. He described Ferry Post as 'the first attempt at the construction of a workable field depot when the only available assets were a patch of sand, an existing or projected railway siding and a length of road'. He went on to stress the availability of space for a then totally unpredictable need for expansion.

The canal area was well suited to this use, having both space and an existing railway running along its length. The then ordnance capability proved sufficient for the first main engagement in the campaign, the Battle of Romani.

Bainbridge describes how the desert railway 'pushed steadily' towards Palestine. One of the defining characteristics of the First World War was rail transport; indeed, an early working title of this volume was *War on Rails*, in contrast to its sister volume, *War on Wheels*. Any map of the Western Front shows a latticework of railway lines bringing essential supplies up to the units. It is not, however, the place of this book to cover rail transport in any detail; it is dealt with more than ably elsewhere.[4] In Palestine, however, the rail network advanced hand in hand with ordnance supply and so offers a thread upon which the narrative may hang.

The starting point of the desert railway was Kantara. Bainbridge describes how this desert station had by 1918 mushroomed into the equivalent of a town with a transient population of 100,000, in comparative military terms the equivalent of Woolwich itself. Based on the canal, it boasted wharves able to service ocean-going vessels, an elaborate shunting yard reminiscent perhaps of Whitemoor, the vast railway junction north of Cambridge. There were then the essential buildings of modern warfare: hospitals, camps, depots, canteens, administrative offices and by-product factories, such as that for soap manufacture in Salonika. All of this on a busy railway junction eventually joining Jerusalem with Cairo; Africa with the east.

The Ordnance depot itself at Kantara was no small beer, having at its height 3,000 personnel initially handling stores from Alexandria but eventually directly from England.

The development from there followed the setting up of railheads at the farthest reaches of the broad-gauge railway line as it was built. The railway was once again the principal organ of communications. It was by train that troops were moved and forage for their horses and food for themselves were transported. The Ordnance use in terms of comparative bulk was small but nonetheless essential. Ammunition was transported by train, as were guns but also uniforms, boots and camp equipment.

The Allied front moved steadily east with the Turks thrown back on a defensive line between Gaza and Beersheba. This stretched the lines of communication and placed heavy demands on Kantara. Most particularly, the supply of Kantara largely by rail from the west of the canal demanded labour-intensive materials handling before stores could be transferred to the desert railway for transporting eastward. The solution found was for stores to come by ship from Alexandria to wharves on the east bank of the canal. This change released much-needed rolling stock for the desert line, greatly speeding up the supply chain.

As always challenges remained. The divisions were advancing faster than the Ordnance infrastructure and over a very broad front. The response was to increase the scale of equipment that a division could hold but also to convert one of the railheads, that at El Arish, into a depot and workshop with one month's supplies.

The increasingly mobile nature of the campaign led to the formation of a Mobile Composite Force in August 1917 comprising an Indian cavalry squadron, Indian infantry and French and Italian contingents. This was supplied by El Arish.

The advance continued and outpaced the new depot, with the result that Kantara once again supplied the new railheads directly.

Ammunition was always separate because of its bulk and nature. Magazines were constructed closer to the advance. The challenge here

Desert train, Omond album. (RLC Archive)

was heat rather than the cold and wet of Flanders. Splinter-proof bays made of timber and sandbags afforded the necessary protection. The nature of the campaign meant that it was not only land forces who demanded supply; 4.5in shells were supplied to the Royal Flying Corps for dropping from aeroplanes.

Once again repair assumed a status of high importance. The distances were simply too great simply to replace damaged articles with new; if something could be repaired, it should be. The terrain in the summer was hard on both boots and wheels. In winter, with the addition of cold and wet, the wear of both multiplied. Boot repairers would go up and down the extended lines. Local people played a large role, not least women who were adept at tent repairs. Workshops were set up to make new wheels and to maintain the heavy guns and vehicles; mobile workshops were also deployed. It was the classic workshop deployment with the major establishment at Kantara, going forward through medium workshops to these mobile units. A snapshot in mid-1917 would have recorded a well-ordered situation serving a large and diverse force of 249,000 British troops, 18,400 Indians and 80,000 Egyptians with 140,000 horses.

The autumn started well with Jaffa falling on 16 November and Jerusalem on 9 December. Winter, though, was another matter altogether.

Uniforms suitable for prevailing weather conditions had to be provided; the extreme heat had changed almost overnight to very cold and wet: men dressed in khaki drill in the desert would find themselves still in khaki drill in the mountains. They had advanced more quickly than the broad-gauge railway could be laid. Torrential rains rapidly converted the desert dust into swamps. The immediate answer to the problem was to link Deir Sineid with the narrow-gauge line built by the Turks, until the new Allied broad-gauge line could be built. The Turkish lines branched northwards to Ludd and east to Jerusalem.

The advance was ever northward and in March 1918 Ludd took over from Deir Sineid as the main advance depot. With the advance came the inevitable litter of salvageable equipment. Bainbridge talks of some 10,000 rifles being recovered in December and January, together with countless old boots, to be repaired and reused.

The object of the advance was, of course, to secure territory and the formerly occupied cities. Bainbridge offers what must have been an eyewitness account of Jerusalem after it fell to the Allies. He writes of its 'closed shops, the utter absence of industrial and social life, and

Desert train, Omond album. (RLC Archive)

Desert supply column. (RLC Archive)

its pallid and furtive population'.[5] It seems that the change brought about by liberation was rapid, with the repair of railways, and, from an Ordnance point of view, the setting up of factories using local labour hungry for work.

Events in northern Europe put a damper if not a complete halt to the advance. The Soviets had taken power in Russia and had withdrawn the Russian armies from the Eastern Front. In order to challenge the redeployment of German troops, British divisions were returned to France and the Palestinian Expeditionary Force took on an altogether different kaleidoscope of Allied nations.

Large numbers of troops came from India and the challenges that Forbes reported with the BEF seem to re-present. Bainbridge writes of them arriving from places as far removed as Aden, India and Mesopotamia, without rifles and camp equipment. Tel el Kebir handled the first rush, but was soon closed down, passing the burden to Kantara. The advance became more 'stately', as Bainbridge puts it: 'we may picture this field depot [at Ludd] in its grove of olive trees, with its lengthy sidings and extensive compound working at full pressure throughout the spring and feeding the right wing [of the front] at

Farriers Suez, Omond album. (RLC Archive)

Jerusalem'.[6] He adds, using very much the language of the time, that there were some '1,000 native labourers including women engaged on tent repair'. The comparative normality is shown also on the Turkish light railway that stretched north to Jaffa where, 'the XXIst Corps had established baths for troops, a clothing disinfecting station and a laundry and repair shop'.

The comparative tranquillity was disturbed by the introduction of long-range guns on the Turkish side. Ludd became too vulnerable to attack and so it was scaled back to a railhead post. At the same time the broad-gauge railway had finally arrived at Jerusalem; the first train from Jerusalem to Cairo ran on 15 June 1918. Now the advancing troops could be supplied from Kantara with railheads at Jerusalem and Ludd. The front had, however, become relatively static and this made it sensible to set up workshops around Jerusalem, Jaffa and Ludd.

The advance recommenced with Damascus falling on 1 October, Beirut on the 6th, Tripoli on the 11th and Aleppo on the 26th, with the armistice with Turkey signed on the 30th. The Ordnance priority now switched to the provision of hospital and other facilities to prisoners and refugees, some 75 per cent of whom required hospital treatment.

MESOPOTAMIA

The Mesopotamian campaign began, Forbes recalls, as an Indian initiative to secure the oilfields of the Persian Gulf. Basra was quickly taken but the comparatively small force met a very much larger Turkish one en route to Baghdad. They sought safety in the city of Kut and after a long and painful siege eventually surrendered on 29 April 1916.

The surrender of Kut triggered the sending by the War Office of British reinforcements. One such was Thomas Cook, a storekeeper and grocer, and who had enlisted in his own trade in Army Ordnance. He served at Le Havre and Abbeville but he was quite adamant that he was not a fighting soldeer. He recalled mounting guard over the first tanks sent to France. His diary continued:

Owing to the heavy losses in the Somme fighting, there was a massive comb-out of men in the service branches of the army to find reinforcements for the depleted infantry regiments. At the same time there was a build-up of the British Forces in Mesopotamia after the ignominious loss of Kut. As this failure had been partly due to poor supply organisation, an important part of the build-up was the creation of adequate supply lines.

Cook was posted to Mesopotamia and his diary records that he spent 11 November 1918 in a tent in Basra in pouring rain listening to the sirens of the craft on the river celebrating the Armistice.[7]

Perhaps a more significant posting was of Brigadier General Hugh Perry, who was sent out as DOS Mesopotamia to take over the Ordnance operation from Indian Ordnance. He notes that among the Indian Ordnance officers left in Mesopotamia was the then Major Routh.

Perry later wrote an account of his time in Mesopotamia and he recalled his first impression of the Basra facilities:

> My first inspection was a most depressing ordeal. The site was constricted and much congested. Everywhere there was a want of neatness and order. This was primarily due to want of supervising staff, but also to want of space, want of labour and want of transport. On the day I went round there were 70 coolies working, the depot could have employed 700.[8]

Probably photographed in Mesopotamia, this Peerless has just started to inch its way across a pontoon bridge. (Richard Pullen)

Perry's response was to up sticks and set up a new depot on a more suitable site. Colonel Howell Jones came with the reinforcements from Egypt and was appointed COO and 'a very fine depot came into being, with excellent sheds and wharves alongside which ocean-going steamers could berth'.

For Forbes much of the story was a repeat of his experience at Marseille in the early months of the war; Indian soldiers were quite simply inadequately equipped for their task. Single fly tents were simply no match for the summer sun and no protection against the winter cold. The Indians used different rifles and so needed different ammunition. With an echo of 1945,[9] the Indians were not warm in their response to British suggestions for better organisation.

The problems did not just extend to the Indians. Perry highlights an issue with rifles. I suspect that this was not unique to Basra, but it seems that the divisions sent out were not all equipped with the same rifles, with a consequent complexity of ammunition supply. Perry addressed the problem by means of a swap between units to ensure that at least all the soldiers in a division had the same rifles.

Perry's report covers a number of other challenges, including the exudation of amatol. The vulnerability of ammunition to extremes of climate has already been mentioned. Perry found that much of the ammunition in Basra had suffered crystallisation and so was useless. The remedy was for the amatol to be emptied from the shells and reground. In order to prevent the problem recurring, Perry adopted a technique developed by Major Campbell in Salonika using paraffin wax. Campbell's expertise with ammunition followed through to the early years of the Second World War.

Another issue concerned winter clothing. The 7th Division reported that it was facing the onset of winter without greatcoats. Perry had found on his arrival at Basra a huge dump of greatcoats but with no indication whence they had come. Two and two were put together and they were returned to their owners.

Boots were a challenge in every campaign. The dry terrain would wear the boots in summer and the cold and wet in winter completed the destructive process. In Mesopotamia the heat would dry out leather, making it completely stiff. The thought of having to change from a pair of boots, that had been worn in, to a new pair was thus a nightmare. The solution was to have boot repairers close to where the troops were, so that boots could be repaired quickly and a pair of soft shoes issued for the brief time the owner was without them.

The state of repair of wagon and gun carriage wheels was far from good. The workshop provision was insufficient to deal with the volume in need of attention and so more skilled wheelwrights needed to be found.

The solution came in the form of the 13th Division. Perry notes that, since this was a relatively new army formation, there were bound to be men of various trades and callings among its ranks. This proved to be the case and soon the 13th's own wheelwrights were repairing some thirty to forty wheels per day.[10]

A related problem was gun springs, where the shortages were acute. Major Wright, who had charge of the workshop, managed to find a blacksmith among the AOC men who had the necessary qualifications to carry out the essential re-tempering of springs.[11] Howell Jones reports that the re-tempered springs were better than the originals. The artificer blacksmith concerned was awarded promotion.

It wasn't just large items: watchmakers had to be found to repair sufficient time pieces in Mesopotamia for zero hour to be set.

One of the soldiers of the 13th Division was Edward Roe. His diary of the campaign records the huge improvement at Basra once the British took control.[12] Perhaps this was just in contrast with what had gone before. For example, Perry records that the Director of Remounts found

Loading munitions, Persian Gulf 1915. (RLC Archive)

3,000 transport ponies 'eating their heads off' and about which no one knew anything.

Nevertheless, in time matters did improve and Perry was appointed to the newly created post of DOS Indian. Brigadier General Charles Mathew succeeded Perry in Mesopotamia and steadily brought to bear lessons learnt in France.

The transport position in Mesopotamia was something of a mirror image of that in Palestine. Mesopotamia was watered by the two great rivers, the Euphrates and the Tigris, of which the Tigris was navigable although with strong currents. Its course would also change after each rainy season. The route from Basra to Baghdad could be made by river but with twists and turns, making it a trip of some 500 miles.

The Allied forces eventually took Baghdad and there is a story that it was an Ordnance officer who was first to enter the city. But it was what the invading troops found that was of greatest interest. In the citadel at the centre of the city there was the armoury for the Turkish troops. It was there that the British found finely engraved swords and rifles; the challenge was how fairly to distribute the spoils, since everyone wanted a souvenir.

ITALY

Italy entered the war on the side of the Allies in May 1915 with the objective of seizing territory from its old rival, Austria. For two years the Italians captured important mountain positions and by 1917 were in a position to try to capture the prize of Trieste.

The British provided ten batteries of 6in howitzers with half an AOC battalion under Lieutenant Colonel Hayley. An Ordnance workshop was set up at Gradisca and a depot, mainly for ammunition, at Palmanova on the ancient border of the Venetian Republic. The plan was for supplies to come from England to Le Havre and thence by rail through to Palmanova. For some reason there was a delay, for the ammunition failed to arrive before 12 May, the day the bombardment was due to start. In the event anything that could be found in the neighbouring area was sent to the forward dumps. In line with Sod's law, almost immediately the supplies arrived from England and thereafter ran smoothly. Trieste, though, was not taken.

Stocks of ammunition continued to grow and in August some 60,000 rounds would have been destroyed in an air raid but for the efforts of Ordnance men in preventing fire spreading from a neighbouring supply depot. Six further howitzer batteries arrived but the plan to take Trieste was abandoned and the number of batteries reduced to just five for defensive purposes only.

The Italians were becoming more and more war weary and on 20 October the Germans reinforced the Austrians and broke through the Italian line, throwing it back on the River Piave with a rendezvous in Treviso. The workshop at Gradisca was abandoned and the contents of the Palmanova depot were estroyed.

Forbes makes a telling point about the Ordnance staff at Palmanova.

> The march of this little band proved a weary business. Most of the men were of low medical category, and those employed as clerks were in no condition to make big physical effort; while, to make matters worse, rain fell in torrents and the road was blocked with traffic.[13]

The British responded with the redeployment of two corps from the Second Army from the Western Front under General Plumer with Haley as his DDOS, who became Director of Ordnance Services for the Italian Expeditionary Force. Bill Williams was appointed DADOS to Italian GHQ at Padua and promoted major on 27 November 1917.[14]

With the risk of Russia leaving the war with its consequent removal of the German Eastern Front, it was always seen as a temporary arrangement with the possibility of the corps being recalled to France to counter the German attack that was expected in spring 1918. Accordingly, ordnance was supplied from the French depots on the basis that no more than one month's supply should be held in Italy. With the length of time it took for supplies to arrive, this was never going to be enough and so, step by step, holdings were slowly built up at Arquata and Rivalta Sriva.

Even the choice of these two places in the north-west of Italy presented problems since most the fighting took place in the east. Accordingly, a depot was set up at Padua, together with a mobile depot.

It had also been decided that no repair workshops were to be set up, with all necessary repair being carried out in France with the return of the damaged equipment. With the sheer volume of clothing requiring repair, again, this simply did not work and so contractors were found in Milan.

There were further challenges for Ordnance. The Line of Communication from the base depot in France now extended to more than 1,000 miles. Ordnance had to provide rest camps and halting places along the way.

Another challenge was similar to that faced in many of the overseas theatres: the variation in terrain and associated weather. Mountain warfare demanded pack saddlery but also alpenstocks, ice axes, snowshoes and skis, sleighs, ice crampons, splinter-proof goggles as protection against rocks fragments, non-freezing oil (something that would also be needed in the Second World War in tanks supplied to Russia), special mule shoes and heavily nailed boots. All this equipment had to be to hand when needed.

Mountains presented huge transport problems, not least for large artillery pieces. The arrangement was that the Italians would provide their own transport and this had to be modified to fit British 18-pounder and 60-pounder guns and 6in howitzers. The 6in mortar was thought to be a very effective mountain weapon but it weighed 170lb. The solution was to cut it in half and once in place fit it back together with a gas-tight joint.

By October 1918 only one corps remained in Italy and this was split and incorporated into the Italian Army, in time for the Armistice on 4 November.

RUSSIA

The Russian Revolution and subsequent treaty of peace signed by the Russian Revolutionary Government forces with Germany at Brest-Litovsk in March 1918 meant that it was only the comparatively small force of White Russians and the rather larger force of Czecho-Slovaks who continued to fight.

Russia had been equipped by the British to a greater or lesser extent from the start and so to continue to supply the White Russians and Czecho-Slovaks was probably inevitable.

In August 1918 a depot was formed at Vladivostok and over the following year some 97,000 tons of arms, ammunition, stores and clothing were provided. It was, by all accounts, a massive operation. Some 200,000 men were clothed and equipped with rifles, machine guns, field artillery, wireless, telegraph and signals stores, transport wagons, harness and saddlery. In terms of quantities, there were 346 million rounds of small arms ammunition, 435,000 blankets, 210,000 sets of clothing, 400,000 sets of Russian underclothing, 300,000 pairs of boots, 1 million hand grenades, 725,000 field dressings, 44,000 sets of harness and saddlery and 1.2 million pairs of horse shoes.[15] The scene was not one of faultless organisation; inadequate accommodation, prisoner of war labour and Russian officials concerned more with their own comfort all posed problems.

In February 1920, the Soviets captured Vladivostok and with it all this equipment, including field guns with Union Jacks painted on them.

On the Black Sea in the south, Lieutenant Colonel Charles de Wolff landed on 6 March 1919 and then commanded a supply depot at Novorossiysk. The depot was ¾ mile from the docks and in six months received 77,000 tons of stores. De Wolff faced immense difficulties in getting reluctant Russians to work; they point blank refused to handle ammunition. In time, though, he created order out of chaos.

When writing *War on Wheels*, I had often wondered how it was that de Wolff seemed to have a background involvement with Russia. In de Wolff's unpublished memoirs of the Second World War there are pictures of him and his wife entertaining and being entertained by Russian officials. In *War on Wheels* he tells of supplies of tanks to Russia being held up in 1941 in order that Russian officials could open crates to inspect the contents. This similar story from de Wolff's time in Novorossiysk may well offer an explanation.

Boxes of different sizes of horse shoes and horse shoe nails arrived in Novorossiysk by their thousands. The Russians were accustomed to opening all boxes of supplies and the horse shoes and nails were no exceptions. De Wolff found piles of horse shoes all mixed up in one room and a massive pile of nails similarly jumbled in the next. It took many man hours to re-sort.

Some 300,000 men were equipped through Novorossiysk, but the depot was abandoned on 26 March 1920 and whatever could be saved was taken to Theodosia in the Crimea.

The third leg of the Russian 'campaign' was more ambitious and involved the landing of a Russian Expeditionary Force in Archangel on the White Sea in June 1918. The force was made up of British, French, Americans, Italians, Russians, Poles, Finns, Serbs and Czecho-Slovaks. The Ordnance staff was small, given the promise that there would be many local Russians ready and willing to help. In October 1918 the major task, being the general distribution of winter clothing, was undertaken. The winter kit had been designed by the explorer

Sir Ernest Shackleton and, with one exception, writes Forbes, was extremely serviceable. The articles consisted of 'blouse, hood and trousers of a light-coloured Burberry material, moccasins for use with snowshoes, fur caps, sheep-skin lined coats, mufflers, sweaters, mitts with gauntlet cuffs, Canadian lumberman's stockings, thick socks, snow-goggles and boots with no iron in their construction'.

The boots were the problem. The absence of iron avoided the conduction of cold, but the leather soles were smooth and so it was difficult to walk on snow and impossible to run. In contrast, Valkani boots, made entirely from blocked felt, were worn by the Russians and performed well in snow. Regrettably not enough of these could be found and so the Shackleton boots were adapted. More regrettably they were adapted by nailing on to the leather soles blocked felt; the nails introduced iron into the boot, necessitating the wearing also of an inner sole to protect against frostbite.

A great many depots were set up and stocked. Repair workshops were set up and equipped. In August 1919 the White Russian troops mutinied and joined the Soviets. All the depots and all the stocks had to be left behind as the Expeditionary Force withdrew. Forbes puts it this way:

> So ended these attempts to fight the Russian revolution. The sole material result of all our efforts was to provide the Soviet Republic with what it most lacked – ample resources of first-rate munitions, military equipment of every kind and splendid clothes for its soldiers.

This rather jumps ahead of the timeline of this book. The import of the Russian Revolution and Russia's effective withdrawal from the Entente was enormous. With peace on the Eastern Front, the Germans could redeploy forces to face the British and the French in the west.

8

THE ROLE OF THE USA

On 6 April 1917 the United States of America declared war on Germany and so joined Britain and the other members of the Entente as a valued ally. Until that point the US government had followed a path of neutrality. That, though, was not necessarily the case with American manufacturers and banks, many of whom did good business supplying the Entente.

Britain had begun the First World War as the undisputed master of the seas. The City of London was where the rest of the world came for banking services: for example, the American cotton crop depended on sterling to finance it. British engineers excelled the world over. Yet American industry was benefitting from the new techniques of mass production and the American economy was ready to make the leap necessary for it to become a superpower.

The declaration of war in August 1914 initially created problems in the USA: would London be able to provide credit for the cotton crop? Worries about the availability of sterling sent the exchange rate higher for a number of weeks. A solution, though, was quickly found.

American businesses quickly settled to the challenge of supplying the combatant nations. Studebaker at South Bend, Indiana, had declared early on that, whilst receptive to them, it would not allow orders from

Entente nations to interfere with its domestic production. It was a major manufacturer of wagons, wheels and saddlery and had set up in Detroit a motor manufacturing subsidiary.

An order had been placed by the British very early on for 3,000 transport wagons. It seems that the order had been fulfilled to everyone's satisfaction and so it was followed in October by a request for 20,000 sets of harness and 60,000 artillery saddles. This was the largest order the company had ever received and well beyond its capacity to fulfil within the timescale set. Accordingly, the Studebaker management contacted other manufacturers and some fifty-three factories got busy with the order. The order was completed in sixteen weeks and the visiting inspectors, 'a fine body of men' including some older cavalry officers, declared themselves satisfied. Further orders followed from all three nations for water carts, artillery wheels, wheel horse harness sets, artillery saddles, ambulance wagons and carts, and Studebaker automobiles.[1]

It is interesting to note a contrasting view from the sharp end of American-supplied equipment, as Omond recorded as he set about equipping his new division for France.

> The Division had been equipped with 1914 pattern leather equipment of American manufacture. It was already evident that this equipment was not fit for overseas work and an Inspector from Woolwich came down on a certain Saturday and condemned it all. It was replaced by an entirely new issue of English make with well-seasoned leather. This experience was not peculiar to this particular division for it had been found necessary in the case of almost every division supplied with American made equipment which had been manufactured and brought over in haste from the United States to help in the time of the great emergency, when this country did not know where to turn for equipment.[2]

There is no record of exactly where the leather equipment to which Omond refers had been made.

In 1912 a debate had been under way amongst American military thinkers concerning the best form of transport in times of war. There were many committed to the mule, as the 3-ton vehicle favoured by the British was thought incapable of working successfully on rough roads. Despite repeated attempts by the Holt Company to demonstrate

Saddlers. (RLC Archive)

the capabilities of tracked vehicles, the Bureau of Ordnance repeatedly declined. This was not the case with the governments of France, Russia and Britain, which had each purchased a number of Holt tractors for the Allied cause.

The Holt Manufacturing Company has already been mentioned in Chapter 6 in relation to the early development of the tank. The Holt Company, in many ways like Hornsby and the other Lincolnshire engineers, was very much part of American agriculture. Its steam tractors and later petrol-driven machines were part of cultivation and harvesting. It was, though, the track-type tractor that was to make such a large contribution to the Allied war effort.

Reynold Wik traces the development of the use of tracks to a Frenchman, D'Herhand, in 1713 and then to Englishman Sir George Cayley in 1825. Benjamin Holt took up the development of the idea and, on Thanksgiving Day, 24 November 1904, Holt's steam engine was given its first field test, where it performed in 'superb fashion'.[3] The rear wheels of the tractor had been replaced by tracks 9ft long and 24in wide with track shoes consisting of 2in by 4in wooden slats. It seems that a painter, Charles Clements, saw the machine and was heard to observe that 'it crawls just like a caterpillar'. The name Caterpillar was registered with the US Patents Office in 1910.

In May 1915 the 75hp Caterpillar crawler was demonstrated at the Rock Island Arsenal in Illinois. It was shown capable of hauling heavy artillery and ammunition through mud where 'neither horses nor any other known motive power could do the job'. The Bureau of Ordnance sought competitive bids for twenty-seven track-type tractors and Holt was the only bidder.[4]

The track-type tractors were tested in anger with the American invasion of Mexico in 1916. General Pershing saw the vehicles cope with desert sand during heavy rain storms and concluded that 'the expedition into Mexico would have been impossible without the tractor and the motor truck'.[5]

The San Francisco Bulletin reported that by September 1916, 1,200 Holt tractors had been shipped to Britain, Russia and France. It is hardly surprising that these huge 'caterpillars' caused a stir when landed in France. *The Autocar Magazine* from 13 November 1915 reported the scene as they were moved to the front:

Tracked tractor with gun. (RLC Archive)

We slip, we skid, we flounder and stick in soft ground. Day begins to dawn. We race the engine. The good old Caterpillar struggles to get away with its load, but the miry ground is too much for her; the gun sticks in the mud. Get all the boys on the rope. Now are we all ready? Race the engine, let in the clutch, and pull with a mighty heave. All together. Heave again. Hurray. Up she comes slowly out of the mud. Uncouple the Caterpillar. Turn the gun around and run her under the trees. Some branches lopped from the trees cover it … It is now daylight but we are safe …

The Holt machine had been demonstrated against the Porsche tractor and an unnamed English tractor in May 1914, both seeking to pull a howitzer 500ft out of a swamp. It seems that it was only the Holt that succeeded. Leo Steiner, the Hungarian farmer who arranged the demonstration, later recalled:

I stood nearby. I heard a shot-like crack, saw the Holt rear up and almost somersault. In the next moment, I saw it return to a horizontal position, lift the gun wheels out of the ground and haul it away. Troops cheered and members of the military committee ran off to offer congratulations.[6]

Tracked gun tractor. (RLC Archive)

Germany's decision not to develop track technology would cost it dear as the British pushed it forward in developing the tank.

Other transportation was less forthcoming for the Allied cause. In his book, *Ford in the Service of America*, Timothy J. O'Callaghan, reminds his reader that Henry Ford was a determined pacifist, so much so that he was heard to comment on the sinking of the RMS *Lusitania*, torpedoed by a German submarine, that the 1,153 people lost 'were fools to go on that boat'. It was known that US shipping, although neutral, was being used to carry munitions to Britain.

On a broader front, American companies had been from the start major providers of what Britain could not provide for herself or from her colonies or allies. America had provided the rifles that the British had not the capacity to manufacture. In 1915, American companies had manufactured 18-pounder high-explosive shells that labour shortages in Britain prevented home-based factories from producing. Bethlehem Steel had provided tons of armour plating and, of course, America had supplied tons of much-needed food.

Up until the time when the USA entered the war, Britain would buy around one quarter of the armaments it needed from the USA. This was massively welcome in helping American business back on its feet following a number of challenging years.

However, initially orders were placed for guns, rifles and ammunition without much consideration given to price and with no coordination between countries or indeed services. This scramble for supplies not only by Britain but by other members of the Entente was also hugely welcome, particularly to Americans who set themselves up as agents. The resulting competition had the effect of driving up prices, much to their benefit. Attempts were made to address this issue from very early on.

Kathleen Burk, in her book, *Britain, America and the Sinews of War 1914–1918*, writes of a conference held on 10 August at which the French proposed that the British should 'take over the purchasing of supplies on behalf of the French government in Britain to avoid bidding and the consequent rise in prices'.[7] This led to the formation of the *Commission Internationale de Ravitaillement*, which eventually covered 'all purchases in Britain and the Empire, and most purchases in Allied countries and in most neutral countries, for France, Belgium, Russia, Serbia, Portugal, Japan, Italy and Rumania'. Britain was regarded in effect as the principal source of not only supply but also of finance, which is discussed later.

The second initiative to stem from the initial scramble was the appointment of the respected New York bankers J.P. Morgan to organise both the finance and purchase of the needs of the British, and so the Entente. The proposition was that, with Morgan as the sole source of orders, the middle man would be cut out along with his percentage and the competition for supplies would be eliminated. As Burk explains, this was all fine in principle, but in practice the Admiralty and the War Office were jealous of their turf and made it clear that they preferred to deal directly with suppliers such as Bethlehem Steel, which manufactured a great many heavy guns for the War Office.

In time and with the urging of Lloyd George, then as Chancellor of the Exchequer, Morgan began to be used more and more. As a banker, Morgan was the first to admit that it knew little of armaments. Accordingly, E.R. Stettinius, the president of the Diamond Match Company, was appointed to coordinate purchasing.[8] In addition, and of vital importance, British inspectors were placed in the major suppliers to ensure the quality of what was being purchased.[9] A third strand, which was to become of even greater importance when America herself entered the war, was the provision of finance by the British to companies to extend their productive capacity. Burk[10] suggests that, amongst others, this virtually created a plant for rifle cartridges and fuses.

The diaries of Lloyd George's Parliamentary Secretary, Dr Christopher Addison, are revealing of some the practical difficulties with the purchasing arrangements.[11] Some 1 million rifles had been ordered, but by May 1916 Lloyd George's papers record that only 480 had been delivered. This figure rose to 200,000 out of 1.6 million by September of the same year. Certainly some of the issues revolved round the inspectors, who demanded a quality in excess of that to which the manufacturers were accustomed to work. The consequent rejects had cost implications and the manufacturers were reluctant to continue. They needed and eventually received financial guarantees.

Another major difficulty was money, not least in 1916 when relations between America and Britain suffered from the strain brought about by events such as the Easter Rising in Ireland and the British attitude to Americans for also supplying the Central Powers. Germany had deep resources from its own industry and reserves of materials and those of the other Central Powers, but was equally able to access the US market for what it needed.

War bonds campaign. (RLC Archive)

As the war progressed, British expenditure mushroomed as its purchases from the USA grew but also as it organised home-grown armament production. The figures were huge; Britain would end up owing the USA $5 billion.[12]

Finance came initially from increases in UK taxation. On 17 November 1914 Lloyd George presented his War Budget, which doubled income tax. The British public was strongly encouraged to do its patriotic duty and invest in war loans; £350 million was raised through the first issue that November. Gold was being mined in a number of the countries within the Empire to help pay for the war effort. However, the British government was not only financing its own expenditure, it was also, to a greater or lesser extent, picking up the tab for its allies. The US government could not lend, even if it wanted to, because of the constraints of neutrality. The British therefore sought and obtained through Morgan borrowings from US banks. Burk writes of the immense efforts of persuasion that were needed but that eventually the largest loan of $500 million had been underwritten by 1,570 bankers – no mean feat.[13]

The more Britain bought from American suppliers, the harder it became to raise the necessary dollar borrowings with which to pay for them. The exchange rate came under pressure and had to be supported if Britain's costs were not to rise even further.

By April 1917 it was thought that Britain had only weeks left before its resources would be exhausted. The declaration of war by President Wilson on 2 April 1917 was thus timely to say the least.

AMERICA AS ALLY

The declaration of war by the USA changed the relationship with Britain from one of supplier and banker to one of ally or partner, or possibly something else. Its impact on the industry, army and people of the United States was a 'slow burn'.

The putative American Expeditionary Force was to be led by General John Pershing, whose name later became attached to a famous Second World War tank. Pershing was a soldier's soldier. He was determined from the start that his men would serve as an American army rather than being dispersed among the Allies and that it would not fall short through want of equipment.

Gilbert records that as early as June 1917 General Pershing was setting up a 'vast apparatus of supply and preparation, essential to ensure American participation in the front line 10 to 12 months hence'.[14] He set up a system to link the ports with the bases and forward depots, and created a General Purchasing Board whose first act was to order 5,000 aircraft and 8,500 lorries from the French authorities.[15] It wasn't just the French, the Ministry of Munitions, now under Churchill, 'was making prodigious efforts to increase British munitions production, as well as manufacturing tanks and aircraft for their new ally'.[16]

In spite of all this activity, the reality of the American army in 1917 was rather different. It was small, with 127,588 officers and men:[17] a fact that, on reflection, is not surprising given the limited need for a large force by a nation defended by sea. The only land war in recent years had been that against Mexico. In 1917, even President Wilson quite possibly had no real idea that the number would increase to 2 million by the end of 1918.

The US War Department was thus geared to support a small army and had done so efficiently for decades. It had a structure of five bureaux, each with a defined remit. The Quartermaster Corps dealt with the food, clothing, shelter and transport of troops; the Corps of Engineers worked with field and coast fortifications, military railways and issued engineering supplies; the Signals Corps handled telegraphy and telephone;

Ordnance handled guns and ammunition; and the Surgeon General's office provide care for the wounded.[18]

The massive growth of the army led to a refocus of the Quartermaster Corps on procurement and supply, with transport and construction split into separate organisations. The country was divided into thirteen areas, General Supply Zones, with each having officers whose role was to procure what was needed from suppliers in their zones. This replaced the previous system which left procurement in the hands of the camp or post Quartermaster.[19]

In his book, *The Army Behind the Army*, E. Alexander Powell offers what is really a wholesale defence of US Ordnance, from which we can infer that in the immediate post-war world criticisms were being bandied around. Powell's thesis, though, is revealing.

In 1917 there were ninety-seven Ordnance officers and men. In the nineteen months during which the USA was at war this figure would increase to 10,000. Powell does, of course, accept that US manufacturers were more than adept at manufacturing pistols, revolvers and rifles. Even to the British, companies such as Remington and Colt were household names. But what of machine guns, howitzers and cannon of all sizes? Powell points out that there was no need for them, certainly on shore; the navy was perhaps another matter. The implication of this was first that, in spite of there being five US Ordnance arsenals, there were not factories ready, waiting and equipped to turn out a massive quantity of weaponry. And a massive quantity would be needed to equip an army of 2 million. It wasn't just the absence of such factories, it was the lack of men with the necessary technical skill. As he points out, ninety-seven does not stretch very far.

To his readers at the time and possibly also to us, the obvious response was that the existing members of the Entente should simply hand over technical drawings and leave the rest to US engineers. However, the Atlantic was becoming infested with enemy submarines. To risk a cargo of raw material was one thing; to risk the loss of many thousands of man and machine hours in turning out the finished product was simply too great a risk. So the common sense solution was to use the armament industries already in place in France and Britain.

The solution eventually adopted was inevitably a compromise, with many supplies coming from British and French armament suppliers, but with a good deal manufactured in the USA.

Henry Ford's stance had remained firmly against war until February 1917 when President Wilson severed diplomatic relations with Germany. 'Well, we must stand behind the President ... In the event of war I will place our factory at the disposal of the United States government and will operate with our one cent of profit.' He added, when the USA declared war on Germany on 2 April 1917, 'I am a pacifist, but perhaps militarism can be crushed only with militarism. In that case I am in on it to the finish.' O'Callaghan observed that: 'The Ford Motor Company would be turned into the arsenal of democracy and Henry Ford was now winning praise from both sides – he had at least tried to end the war with his peace mission and now he was a realist supporting the war. Some now call him "the fighting pacifist".'[20] His exaggerated boasting about the number of submarines, tanks and motors that he could produce perhaps underpinned this title.

The first priority was to address the food shortage in Britain. Accordingly, work began on tractor design and prototypes were shipped in January 1917. Some 7,000 tractors had been sent by April 1918. A further 27,000 tractors were supplied to farmers in Canada and the USA,[21] all with a focus on food production for the Allies.

With the onset of war, Ford domestic car production reduced to small hundreds and capacity was redirected towards the war effort. Some 2,397 ambulances, designed by Ford in collaboration with the US Surgeon General's office, were supplied to the Red Cross, with a

Model T Ford ambulances. (Richard Pullen)

further 5,745 supplied to the army along with 16,899 passenger cars, 7,490 trucks and 600 chassis.[22] Of the vehicles used by the American Expeditionary Force in France, 20,652 had been made by Ford and 18,039 by others.[23]

The US contribution to air warfare was directed at training planes. Ford had the option of seeking to copy one or more of the sixty different European aircraft engines then in use. The Ford engineers contemplated the prospect of converting the hand-making process of such engines with metric measurement into something that could be handled by Ford production methods, but concluded that it would be altogether more satisfactory to start from scratch with an American design. Thus the Liberty Aircraft engine was born and production began in August 1917. This engine would go on to power the Liberty Tank.

The production of Eagle boats for the navy was the most substantial of all Ford's contributions. The Eagle was an all-steel submarine chaser, vital in seeking to protect the convoy of merchant ships laden with munitions and food to Britain.

Of technical, if not numerical, interest, the Ford tank appeared in 1917. These were much closer to the 6-ton two-man tank produced by Renault than the monstrous British 14-tonners that succeeded in being effective against German machine guns. Ford produced some fifteen 2½-ton tanks armed with a machine gun and powered by two model T engines, 'locked together and synchronised so that if one engine failed the other could still run both tracks'.[24] This 2½-tonner was succeed by a 3-ton and a 6-ton version, neither of which was ready for action before the Armistice.

Of greater numerical significance, Ford produced 2.7 million metal helmets that had the huge advantage of weighing only 2lb.

Ford plants in Britain and elsewhere in Allied countries outside the USA were brought into war production from 1914. In Britain they 'built over 30,000 Model T troop carriers, water carriers, ambulances and munition carriers as well as an unknown quantity of shell casings'.

The author of *GM: The First 75 years of Transportation Products*, reported that:

Between 1917 and 1919 90 per cent of GM's truck production was directed to war manufacturing, and the division sent 8,500 trucks to the Armed Forces. Cadillac supplied 2350 army staff cars, 1157 artillery tractor V-8 engines, trench mortar shells at a rate of 20000 rounds a day, and a large number of specialized military vehicles based on the V-8 145 in chassis that included America's first full armoured car.[25]

He went on to explain that America's entry into the war effectively removed the distinction between military and domestic production. Motor companies such as GM were well able to do both:

> The automobile industry, with no previous experience in military manu-
> facture, completed within only 18 months an outpouring of weaponry
> that is credited with winning the war, changing the face of Europe and
> giving rise to the US as a world power.[26]

The variety of what poured out of the GM plants was huge and included 'field kitchen trailers, airplane engines and a varied array of military supplies un-thought of as the purview of automobile manufacturers – such as 820,000 steel helmets'.

THE BRITISH MISSIONS TO THE USA

One of the first acts of the British government following the entry of the USA into the war was to send a mission lead by Foreign Secretary Balfour. The mission was large and covered a wide range of areas where discussion was needed. The army mission was led by General Tom Bridges, who was then still in command of the 19th Division in France. He was accompanied by a team that included Captain T. Heron of the Army Ordnance Department, who ran the Northern Line of Communication in France. The Ministry of Munitions was represented by its Director of Requirements. Other missions covered shipping, food, transport and finance.

Bridges sought first to get the US Army to adopt the standard issue of British weapons, not least the rifle, with huge potential benefits to the supply chain. The Americans declined, preferring to stay with their .30 rimless cartridge.

Remington and the other well-known small arms manufacturers had been producing quantities of Royal Enfield rifles to the British design since October 1914. These were .303s and were standard throughout the British Army. Bridges' request was thus not unreasonable. The objection Powell cites is the fact that US ammunition was of .30 calibre and rimless, unlike the British .303. He explores the options and supports the conclusion made by US Ordnance that the best plan was to take the Royal Enfield design and amend it to take .30 ammunition.

The question of the machine gun and automatic rifle led on from this and was revealing in a different way. The US company, Browning, had designed and was producing a machine gun. This compared favourably with the Lewis gun, the much heavier Vickers and the French Hotchkiss. It is easy to see that Powell has something of a passion for US arms when he describes the Browning as 'the most efficient weapon of its type'.[27] On a more practical level, he talks of its production and how capacity was increased by engaging other gun manufacturers such as Winchester. So once again, American design prevailed.

Notwithstanding controversies, it is clear that US industry did indeed step up to the mark, as Powell illustrates with some astonishing statistics. He takes the period from 6 April 1917 to 11 November 1918 and small arms ammunition. The US Army used 2,879,148,000 rounds compared to 3,486,127,000 for Britain and 2,983,675,000 for France.[28] He makes the point that the latter two had by then an established industry, which makes the American production all the more commendable. We might, though, recall the assistance given by Britain in massively supporting the American ammunition industry.

Bridges' second and more urgent request was for American soldiers to join British divisions as soon as possible to make up for manpower shortages resulting from the horrific losses on the Somme and at Verdun. Again the Americans declined. It seems that Pershing was determined to stick to his plan of wholly American divisions. They did, however, promise to dispatch a regular division to France to support the French and more immediately to send 'a number of railway battalions to man the supply line in France, medical units, including six base hospitals, and trained and untrained pilots for the Air Service'. In addition, companies of foresters were sent to fell timber for the trenches and soldiers' quarters.[29]

The finance element of the mission was led by accountant Hardman Lever. He was a tough negotiator and had not endeared himself to US Treasury Secretary McAdoo. This less than cordial relationship made it difficult for Britain to secure the constant stream of finance that it needed. Dogged determination and probably the absence of any alternative resulted in finance being secured regularly at the last minute. McAdoo would constantly be reminded that, more and more,

US industry was dependent on war production and so providing finance to Britain to enable it to order ever larger quantities made economic sense. The strain on the American financial system was huge, with the US Government itself raising a $2,000 million 'Liberty Loan'[30] intended for its own expenditure.

The Balfour mission was followed by a mission led by the newspaper magnate Lord Northcliffe and then by the man who would become British ambassador, Lord Reading. The Reading mission included economist J.M. Keynes, who headed up the section of the Treasury dealing with inter-allied finance.[31] Behind the leading men of both missions were serving soldiers, who joined a growing British Army presence in the USA with the role of oiling the wheels of war. One such was Tom Leahy.

Leahy[32] took his experience of war to the USA as an adviser on matters of supply to the US Ordnance Department and he kept a record of some of what he did.

On one occasion, he attended a speech given in Chicago by British Lieutenant Colonel G.G. Woodward to the Convention of the American Bankers' Association. This rather odd match of soldier and banker is made rather less odd when remembering the continuous difficulties the British had of financing their expenditure in the USA and the corresponding vital role of bankers.

Leahy recalled that Woodward began by telling how the British and Commonwealth armies came into being and how we 'built a fighting machine which has enlisted no less than 8,500,000 souls – of which total Great Britain herself has contributed 6,250,000; the Dominions 1,000,000; India and the Dependences 1,500,000. Today one out of every three males, of all ages, in the British Isles is fighting.'[33] He went on to explain the complexities and demands on supply. The response of the bankers is not recorded.

On a more bizarre note, Leahy recalled an article in the *Washington Star* of 18 October 1918 with the headline, 'Experts will fit army shoes, socks'. The article went on to explain that 'the conservation of foot energy of the soldier is a problem that has for years perplexed the War Department'. The solution was that 'a detachment of foot fitting experts may be attached to every regiment or division … measurements will be taken and shoes fitted as soon as practicable after the soldier enters service'. Again, Leahy's response is not recorded.

The principal task allotted to Leahy and his small team in the USA was to catalogue all the items provided by Ordnance Services. In doing this he visited the ports of debarkation and explosives depots, and also armouries and arsenals. The catalogue would list all items with brief descriptions of weight and size and also price, for valuation purposes. It is clear that the plan was for the catalogue to be updated frequently. The task was due to have been completed by August 1918, but it is not recorded whether it ever was.

The compilation of the catalogue must have been tedious in the extreme, especially for a young man keen to do his bit. Leahy had done his, but those working for him perhaps had not. There is on file a very sad letter from Leahy to the father of one such young man. It talks of the son being assigned to the cataloguing task and of the son saying to Leahy, 'Colonel you know this is not the kind of job I joined the army for.' Leahy sympathised and added that, 'the first duty of a soldier is to do what he is assigned to do, as well and as cheerfully as he possibly could'. He went on to say that he promised to find him an overseas posting at the earliest possible opportunity. He tells of the warm send-off the son was given. The letter ends with Leahy's sympathy to the father at the news that, following the overseas posting, his son had died from pneumonia.

The efforts of men such as Leahy and Bridges, of US industry and Ordnance, equipped some 2 million American soldiers who crossed to France before the Armistice.

At the beginning of 1918 with the Germans moving their eastern army to the Western Front, none of this was moving fast enough for General Bridges. He was part of the Reading Mission and continued to argue for American troops to join their British and French counterparts as soon as possible.[34]

9

THE END

Captain Omond's correspondence book from 17 January 1918[1] opens with a commonplace request; it was for a replacement carriage for a 4.5in howitzer that had become unserviceable through hostile fire. It reports that this was ready for issue on 20 January. The next few days' entries concern correspondence with the COO at Calais from which it might be reasonable to infer that the latter was being a stickler over issues to the Portuguese divisions. Omond was still DADOS to the Portuguese.

Leafing through to 17 March, Omond wrote that he had success-fully completed his course and hoped to be 'gazetted as 4th class O.O. [Ordnance Officer] and told to proceed to HQ 1st Army. He arrived on 22 March and in his book reported on changes at the top: 'Colonel Forbes is going to Mesopotamia, General Parsons is taking Stevens' place at the War Office and Mathew is returning from Mesopotamia to become DOS France.'

The next day, 23 March 1918, everything changes.

The fighting in the South is not going at all well … apparently there have been no lines to fall back on and it is difficult to see where we are going to stop.

24 March: The Boches are liking this weather – apparently they have crossed the SOMME and are well beyond PERONNE. No doubt our excellent system of light railways and roads are helping them. It is unpleasant news these days, but we can but fight on.

On 1 April he wrote that they received a visit from representatives from the DOS to 'see how we are getting on' and four days later Omond reported that General Gough has been sent home, adding that 'many people think this might have been done in August last year on account of the muddles made by the 5th Army in Belgium'. He also added that 'Foch is now Generalissimo – not surprising in view of all that has happened.'

The volume ends on 17 April with Omond reporting that what remained of the 16th Division was digging its last line of defence, adding that 'it is rather sad after all the old days'.[2]

The significance of 23 March was that Thursday, 21 March 1918 saw the breakthrough of Allied lines by the Germans, now reinforced by those redeployed from the Eastern Front. An attack had been expected and the Allies had been bracing themselves. Forbes describes how the German attack, with highly trained and rested storm troopers and machine gunners, overwhelmed the British lines, outnumbering them by as much as three to one.

The Fifth Army on the Somme had no choice but to fall back; the Third Army followed suit.

The German advance, however, became bogged down as supplies struggled to get through the desolation caused by years of shell fire. Far from helping, the light railway track possibly got in the way. Lorries broke down and blocked tracks; wagons became stuck in mud. Forbes adds that not even the superior German organisation could overcome these impediments.

In contrast, the British fell back on land as yet untouched by war, but also on rear supply dumps, enabling them to set up gun positions with ample supplies of ammunition. Also, troops could be redeployed across the whole line of defence. The main breakthrough on 21 March threatened Amiens with all its rail infrastructure. Further major breakthroughs took place on 28 March and 9 May, threatening both Paris and the Channel ports. In no case did the Germans fully succeed, although the fighting was hard and the loss of life and injury dreadful, for both defender and attacker.

The Contemptible Little Army back in 1914 had been a mobile army equipped with nothing it could not take with it. The years of trench warfare had changed all that. Mobile workshops, brought up close to the guns they were to maintain, had taken root. Workshop lorries had attracted collections of temporary but immobile structures. More and more heavy machinery had been brought up; it was after all more efficient. Ordnance officers attached to units prided themselves on being able to supply what was needed when it was needed; their dumps had grown. Ammunition was needed in ever increasing variety and quantity; indeed, finding space for its storage far to the rear was becoming more of a challenge and so more was stored ready for use close to those who needed it.

All this meant that for Ordnance the retreat was a nightmare, given the need either to take with them all the workshops, equipment, stores and ammunition they could, or, failing that, to destroy them to deny the enemy.

Dumps closest to the front were simply overrun and the stores and ammunition lost. Further back were the railheads.

After Gallipoli, Captain Comley Hawkes had moved with the 29th Division to France, where he took part in the Battle of the Somme. He was commissioned in the field on 25 May 1917.

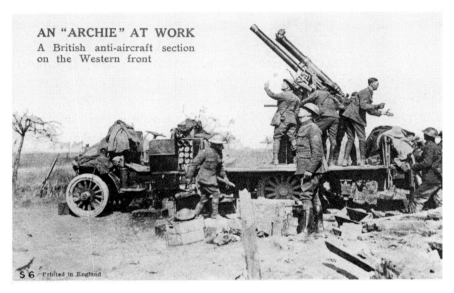

AN "ARCHIE" AT WORK
A British anti-aircraft section on the Western front

Anti-aircraft gun on the Western Front. (RLC Archive)

Comley Hawkes' diary[3] described the three days during which he and those under his command worked hard under fire to evacuate valuable ordnance stores away from the German advance. This is how he described the closing stages:

When I got back to Rocquigny the rattle of machine guns could be heard quite distinctly in the valley and soon a staff Major said, 'you had better clear out as the Bosche are in Manancourt (about 2 miles away)'.

This would be about 11.30 am and there was no engine on the train as it had gone to Le Plateau to get some water. [Hawkes and his men had loaded trucks with the stores to be evacuated at the railhead]. So I got my men together and saw that they had a good supply of ammunition.

We could see that the Bosche were advancing fast and the 18 pdrs were well behind us firing over our heads and the rattle of machine guns came nearer every minute.

In the nick of time the old engine came and, after a bit of shunting, we pulled out about 2 pm while the enemy were in the wood by Le Mesnil, thus overlooking the railhead.

However, we got away without a casualty and picked up my other men at Le Transloy.

When we got down to Mahault we found all the people there packing up (some fifteen miles away from the line).

I intended to make my dump at Edge Hill but found that was impossible and tried to get in touch with Army Headquarters, but without success.

There was only one thing to do i.e. to go on to Romes Camp, so we kept on the train …

We reached Romes Camp about 4.30pm on Sunday [the next day] and immediately went to the Ordnance Depot to see if I could get through to Headquarters and find out what were my instructions.

The O.O. could not be found as I suppose it being Sunday he was having it off, but finally he was forthcoming and seemed very upset at having to work.

He gave us no kind of help to get any food; in fact, it seemed that he and his staff did not know that there was a war going on, as they were about 45 miles from the front.

We made the best of it by borrowing three tents in which we may rest ourselves and put things straight after 4 days battle.

Instructions were now issued that we were to go to Etaples for a few days' rest.

Captain Hawkes was awarded the Military Cross by the Commander in Chief, two of his sergeants received Military Medals, and Certificates were awarded to a private and a lance corporal. Hawkes' clerk, Private Morris, he described as 'indeed a marvel and throughout showed such a disregard for danger that is not often met with'.

Forbes offers a number of accounts where Ordnance men showed great courage in evacuating all they could.

No. 7 Medium Workshop at Matigny was under the command of Captain Dowling, who received the order to 'quit' on 21 March. By working through the night, they were ready to move off the next day. For eight days they travelled the countryside, picking up abandoned equipment en route, and it was only on 29 March at Poix that they were again fully operational, repairing a large number of siege howitzers. Other accounts tell of workshops making repairs under heavy fire. Forbes does add though that, had mobile workshops remained fully mobile as intended, they would have been able to move faster and be back in operation far more quickly.

It was not only repair, but also supply. The activities of the Fifth Army park at La Flaque were recorded by Captain Guy, the officer in charge. With the German offensive, the demand for guns of all kinds was huge and it looked as if the park would run out. Fortune came in the form of a sixty-truck train, which provided enough for five days. On 26 March the guns had set up positions to the rear of the park and it was time to move, which they did first to Longeau. With further heavy fire, the park, still issuing guns and spares, moved back to Poix. It came finally to rest on 9 May at Pont Remy. In its retreat it had issued 585 guns and 2,941 machine guns.[4]

The orders for Ordnance officers in charge of ammunition dumps were to stay with them until the last possible minute and then to destroy what could not be moved. The OXF 'Trent' ammunition depot is an example offered by Forbes. On 9 April a good part of its large reserve had been set alight by shell fire and for some five hours the fire had to be battled to save the remainder of the ammunition. Forbes tells how Captain Gee had come from Army HQ to lead the fight. Gee had the rare distinction among ordnance men of having an Military Cross with two bars each awarded for gallantry. Captain Alaway, the officer in charge, takes up the story:

During the afternoon of the next day it became apparent from the heavy traffic retiring towards Bailleuil that something untoward was happening, and this was confirmed by explosions at O.X.D. [the depot] three kilometres away toward Armentieres. I therefore detailed my party, who were to destroy the dumps, to be in readiness. At about 2pm the commander of B/121 Brigade RFA [Royal Field Artillery] galloped in and enquired if any 18-pounder or 4.5 inch ammunition was available and the quantity. I informed him that far more was available than would meet his immediate requirements. Shortly after this a number of limbers pulled into the depot and refilled. At 3pm some field batteries took up positions at the far end of the depot and immediately went into action. At 5pm the RE destroyed the railway opposite. At about 7.30 the crisis passed and my party, who had remained in readiness the whole time to fire the depot, was dismissed.[5]

The account continued, telling how issues kept being made under heavy fire right up until one hour before the depot was finally evacuated and the remaining stock destroyed.

Forbes estimates that some 100,000 tons of ammunition and other stores were lost in the retreat. He goes on to say that it was always better to have too much rather than too little in hand and so losses in retreat were inevitable. However, he does caution again that, had ordnance remained more mobile, the losses would have been reduced. This has to be set against the fact that ammunition reserves far exceeded that which could be held on trains. Also, the policy of moving more and more to transport by light railways resulted in there being insufficient lorries to evacuate great quantities of stores.

The Ordnance aspect was, of course, but a small part of the retreat.

The German advance of March 1918 provided an opportunity for the new light Whippet tanks to show their paces. The 19th Division had been ordered to concentrate on Hebuterne in the early hours of 26 March. The move was successful and by 1 p.m. there was in place 'a continuous line of troops from Gommecourt to Souastre'.

Some excitement was caused during the afternoon by the sight of a battalion of Whippet Tanks covering the advance of the Anzacs, who were moving up to relieve the Division. This was the first appearance in the field of these new steel engines of war; they were of much lighter build than the ordinary tank and more mobile. As no notification had been received

A factory shot of the Medium A Whippet tank from 1918. (Richard Pullen)

The identity and location of this Mk IV are unknown. Note the amount of petrol tins, track extensions and general debris carried on top. (Richard Pullen)

warning the troops of these new tanks, some guns were moved forward to deal with them should they prove hostile; one RA patrol definitely reported them as German tanks.[6]

It wasn't only Whippets. Heavy tanks were to play a significant role in the counter-attack.

The German advance not only overran the front line, it put into threat the rear ammunition depots. Orders had been issued to the ammunition depots concerning what they had to do in the event of retreat. A copy of one such order is in the RLC archive for the Blargies Nord depot, 12 Ordnance Depot. A sharp distinction is made between preparing and destroying, the latter only taking place on an order given in writing. Preparation may have taken between twelve and eighteen hours, whereas destruction would take only two. In the event the German advance came within 28 miles of the depot and indeed some batteries came to it to draw ammunition directly. The written order was never issued.

Under threat also were the massive depots at Le Havre and Calais. Forbes suggests that this highlighted the folly of having so much in France. He acknowledges, though, the obvious advantages of saving potentially dangerous trips across the Channel to repair uniforms, for example, which were being cheaply and effectively repaired by French women workers in Ordnance workshops and local factories. Le Havre and Calais were not only well stocked, probably overstocked, but they were also the place where salvage in transit would pause on its journey to be repaired and reissued. There were thus mounds of clothing, blankets, shell cases and endless other items. They were effectively stuck in France because of the shortage of ships crossing the Channel but also because of the shortage of storage back home.

It remains a mystery why these lessons so hard learnt had been forgotten by 1939 with the result that vast stores and many thousands of vehicles were left behind at Dunkirk.[7]

With the threat to Le Havre and Calais, the smaller depot at Abbeville became more and more a centre of activity.

The war diary of 8 AOD at Abbeville for April 1918, confirms this. The author, Fairholme, had by then been promoted to major.[8]

On 1 April the key concern was the ability of 8 AOD to supply the needs of the Fifth Army. Issues were made of boots, socks, shirts, horse shoes, oil, flannelette and blankets. Also issued were limbered wagons, travelling kitchens, 3in trench mortars, machine guns, steel helmets, Hotchkiss and Lewis guns for anti-aircraft defence, tents and field dressings.

The large amount of repair work to vehicles meant that tables and trestles were having to wait. It was apparent that in more 'normal times' large numbers of such items had been issued on a regular basis:

> Further issues were made of water carts, bicycles, 50,000 rounds of small arms ammunition.

> Ten Lewis guns were issued to Chinese labour companies for use against aircraft (subsequently cancelled).

The diary is quite frank in places:

> Truck with about 15 tons of machinery arrived addressed to 8 Ordnance Workshops. Not for this Depot, telephoned Havre and Director Ordnance and cannot obtain any information as to whom it is for.

> Machine gun fitted to commandant's motor car as an experiment.

> 500 rifles and bayonets issued to 24th Division. Artillery and Field Companies of 52nd Division being equipped.

There is a good deal in the diary about wheels, which came in a number of different classes: e.g. 3rd class B No. 150; 2nd class C No. 200. Abbeville did, after all, supply the advance horse transport depot nearby.

The German advance eventually came to a halt and the Allies, now with American reinforcements and all under the command of Marshal Foch, began their own advance toward Germany. Forbes writes of the Germans as a broken army with morale at an inevitably low ebb; the much-vaunted offensive had failed.

For Ordnance, the American battalions, which were to join British divisions, had to be equipped as their British colleagues; later, once the American Expeditionary Force began to operate as such, this equipment was returned and replaced by US-style issue.

The Battle of Amiens in August, which began the Hundred Days Offensive, saw tanks in great numbers leading the attack followed closely by the infantry. This proved successful, although the fighting was still gruelling and costly.

Abbeville. (RLC Archive)

Devastation in France. (RLC Archive)

Ordnance was now mobile again, and workshop and stores lorries would advance behind the line in pairs, so that while one was in use, the other was moving forward.

Back in Abbeville in August 1918, the war diary reveals a variety of activity.[9] The presence and needs of prisoners of war figure more prominently, as does the role of Chinese labour. As September comes, there are notes of supplies being returned to UK depots. Vehicles were to be returned to England for repair, but wheels were to be kept for reuse in France.

In the higher reaches of the command structure, the talk was of preparation for a massive offensive in 1919. The Americans would be fully ready by then; thousands of tanks would have been manufactured and committed to the field. The armaments industry was working at full pace, notwithstanding growing labour unrest, possibly inspired by the Russian Revolution.

In September 1918 the Allies assembled a phenomenal resource for a planned attack on the St Mihiel salient. Gilbert describes the preparations. 'Some 3,000 guns and 40,000 tons of ammunition had been brought together. By then the certainty of heavy casualties was fully accepted and sixty-five evacuation trains had been prepared with 21,000 hospital beds. Fifteen miles of road had been constructed and 300 miles of standard

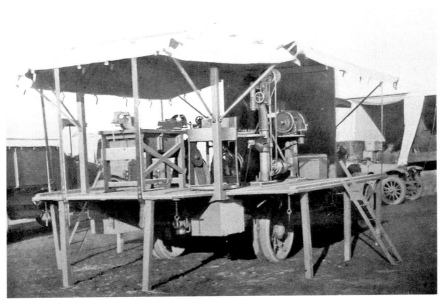

The Daimler mobile workshop in its operational form. (Richard Pullen)

and light gauge railway had been built.'[10] Over the previous four years many mistakes had been made, much ingenuity employed and Ordnance Services had learnt much from all of these. At last, the Ordnance supply machine seemed to be working.

The prize fighters, the Entente and the Central Powers, were however reeling from each other's blows. The whole population of nations were either fighting or making armaments, or working in some way for the war effort. In spite of the positive messages put out by the German high command, the reality was of exhaustion. Other members of the Central Powers were exhausted too; Turkey and Austria were seeking peace. As Forbes suggests, Germany had, by throwing its best at the Western Front in the spring of 1918, in effect defeated itself.

The Armistice was signed on 11 November 1918.

A short walk through the Commonwealth Graves in Lincoln, and I suspect many other places, reveals the tragedy that, notwithstanding the Armistice, it was not all over. Young men continued to die. It would be some eight months until the peace was signed, on 19 July 1919.

Salvage. (RLC Archive)

The process of demobilisation caused huge problems for thousands of ordinary soldiers. The government decided that priority should be given to those men in pivotal occupations. So coal miners, for example, came first. The problem was that many of these had been conscripted only recently and so those volunteers who had served from the start or at least from early on felt seriously aggrieved.

For the men of the AOC it was, if anything, worse. Since the AOC had the job of clearing up, its men would be the last to leave. In the last two years of the war its ranks had been cleared of those fit for the front line and replaced with the wounded and disabled, whose claim to early discharge was even stronger. It took a revolt in one of the workshops for the government to see the error of its ways, and length of service was adopted as a key criterion.

Demobilisation, irrespective of the order in which it took place, would take many months and Ordnance faced a massive demand for tents and bedding for the army to be able to make the months of waiting as bearable as possible. The depots provided refresher courses in tradesmen skills that might have grown rusty in the years of war. Other courses were provided in draftsmanship and mathematics, but also cultural subjects such as English literature and history. Although men worked while they were waiting, the most arduous work was given to German POWs and, jarringly in twenty-first century eyes, to Chinese coolies.[11]

Alongside demobilisation of men came the need to clear the materiel of war from massive tracts of land. There were depots still filled with all manner of stores. Each soldier had his kit, of which he would only keep uniform and boots. It was a challenge of many thousands of tons.

It wasn't just British equipment; the Germans had left tons of their own in retreat. Forbes[12] highlighted some twenty barges found filled with German machine guns. The Ministry of Munitions set up a Disposals Board to find uses for items from railway engines to millions of knives, forks and spoons.

Ammunition was a whole different matter. The estimate here was of 350,000 tons of ammunition left in trenches, gun positions, forward dumps, roadside dumps, railheads and depots. The ammunition was of all kinds and, to make matters worse, German ammunition was not well understood and so had to be investigated and learnt. Incredibly, only four fatalities were recorded.

It was a painstaking process. Each shell had to be taken apart by hand and its constituent parts separated for reuse wherever possible. Again, the Ministry of Munitions set up an organisation, the Directorate of Munitions Recovery. An article that appeared in the *Cologne Post* spoke of 3,500 acres piled high with ammunition. It gave an illustration of one dump of 60,000 6in shells that contained 2,300 tons of steel, 20 tons of copper and more than 240 tons of high explosive. The high explosive would be separated into TNT, which had to be destroyed, and ammonium nitrate, which was used in fertiliser to begin to restore the fields of Flanders.

Captain Omond was one of those going home and he ends his account with this personal reflection:

> Many efforts have been made to picture in words the awful destruction wrought by the German fiends on the fair countryside and industrial areas of France and Belgium. But, though some of the writing is both graphic and picturesque, it does not produce the atmosphere of somber awfulness which hangs over ruined Ypres and shattered Lens.
>
> In the same way, it is doubtful if any pen can ever describe with any touch of reality the amazing contrasts which were to be found in and near the battle front. On the one hand, there was the wonderful comfort of DHQ and, perhaps less than five miles away, the filth and discomfort of the trenches.
>
> There were the clean habitués of the regions further back to contrast with the mud-spattered, battle-stained warriors of the front line, risking their lives every minute of the day. There were the leave trains full of hail and hearty men, and the ambulance trains carrying the sick and wounded back to 'Blighty': It was all war, of course, and everybody was but a cog in the machinery, which was to drive the German to his knees begging for armistice.[13]

The officers and men of Army Ordnance clearly had conducted themselves with distinction since, after the war, General Sir Travers Clarke, Quartermaster General for France, had this to say about the corps: 'Ordnance was the ever-present help of the British soldier in an ordeal of unexampled severity.' The Army Ordnance Corps was rewarded in 1918 by the addition of the word 'Royal' to its name.

Following the long process of salvage, an RAOC presence remained in Germany supporting the British Army of the Rhine. Bill Williams returned following postings in Stirling and Gibraltar and was the last Ordnance officer to leave when everything that remained was brought home in 1929.

In trying to make any assessment of what had been learnt it is necessary to make the impossible jump into the minds of soldiers in the late 1920s.

Evacuation of the British Army of the Rhine in 1929. (Bill Williams Archive)

Did they even contemplate then that within a decade it might all happen over again?

The men and women who had equipped the army moved mountains. In August 1914, I believe that no one had had any real idea of what lay ahead. The carnage was unforgivable; a whole generation lost.

The achievement of those engaged in supply was, though, remarkable. It gave the fighting men the tools they needed to do the job. It had other positive outcomes; war does force-feed technology, and that technology can be used in peace as in war. Work conditions were in many places transformed, with previously unheard of works canteens, for example. Women had witnessed their own potential, though tragically many would have to wait until after another war before they could fulfil it.

Lessons were learnt, though many seemingly as quickly forgotten. One can speculate endlessly why this might be. One reason surely was that they had been through hell and had no intention of returning.

NOTES

Chapter 1

1   *War on Wheels*, Philip Hamlyn Williams, The History Press, 2016, p.36.
2   *History of the Army Ordnance Services*, Forbes, Vol.3, Medici, 1928, p.13.
3   *First World War*, Martin Gilbert, Harper Collins 1995, p.55.
4   *First World War*, Martin Gilbert, Harper Collins 1995, p.43.
5   *The Great Munition Feat 1914–1918*, George A.B. Dewar, Constable and Company, 1921, p.9.
6   *A Short History of the Army Ordnance Dept*, Royal Arsenal and Dockyard, Woolwich, RLC Archive.
7   *History of the Army Ordnance Services*, Forbes, Vol.3, Medici, 1928, p.19.
8   *A DADOS in France*, Lieutenant J.S. Omond, RLC Archive, p.18.
9   Lecture on the Army Ordnance Department, its organisation and duties at home and in the field delivered to Officers of Staff Courses, Clare College, Cambridge by Lieutenant Colonel T.B.A. Leahy, 30 September 1916, RLC Archive.
10 *War on Wheels*, Philip Hamlyn Williams, The History Press, 2016, p.11.
11 *OC Workshop Gazette*, RLC Archive.
12 *History of the Army Ordnance Services*, Forbes, Vol 2, Medici, 1928, p.95.
13 *To the Warrior His Arms*, Steer, Pen & Sword, 2005, p.10.
14 *AOC Workshop Gazette*, RLC Archive.
15 *AOC Gazette*, 15 August 1914, RLC Museum.
16 IWM recordings.
17 *The Wheelwright's Shop*, George Sturt, Kindle edition.
18 *To the Warrior His Arms*, Steer, Pen & Sword, 2005, p.12.
19 *History of the Army Ordnance Services*, Forbes, Vol.3, Medici, 1928, p.3.
20 *History of the Army Ordnance Services*, Forbes, Vol.3, Medici, 1928, p.19.

21 Bill Williams archive.
22 *History of the Army Ordnance Services*, Forbes, Vol.3, Medici, 1928, p.22.
23 *First World War*, Martin Gilbert, Harper Collins 1995, p.60.
24 *The Diary of an Old Contemptible*, Kindle edition, loc. p.759.
25 *History of the Army Ordnance Services*, Forbes, Vol.3, Medici, 1928, p.21.
26 *History of the Army Ordnance Services*, Forbes, Vol.3, Medici, 1928.
27 *History of the Army Ordnance Services*, Forbes, Vol.3, Medici, 1928, p.25.
28 *History of the Army Ordnance Services*, Forbes, Vol.3, Medici, 1928, p.28.
29 *History of the Army Ordnance Services*, Forbes, Vol.3, Medici, 1928, p.31.
30 *History of the Army Ordnance Services*, Forbes, Vol.3, Medici, 1928, p.15.
31 *History of the Army Ordnance Services*, Forbes, Vol.3, Medici, 1928, p.28.
32 *Railways of the Great War*, Colette Hooper, Bantam Press, 2014, p.55.
33 *The Mobilization of British Army Logistics for the First World War*, Major W.E. Campbell, RLC Archive.
34 *History of the Army Ordnance Services*, Forbes, Vol.3, Medici, 1928, p.37.
35 *History of the Army Ordnance Services*, Forbes, Vol.3, Medici, 1928, p.38.
36 *Arms and the Wizard*, R.J.Q. Adams, Texas A&M Press, 1977, p.6.
37 www.cwgc.org/find-a-cemetery/cemetery/90801/ST.%20SYMPHORIEN%20MILITARY%20CEMETERY
38 *First World War*, Martin Gilbert, Harper Collins 1995, p.61.

Chapter 2

1   *A DADOS in France*, Lieutenant J.S. Omond, RLC Archive.
2   *The Royal Arsenal Woolwich*, Welsey Harry, 1987, p.14.
3   *The Royal Arsenal Woolwich*, Welsey Harry, 1987.
4   *History of the Army Ordnance Services*, Forbes, Vol.2, Medici, 1928, p.107.
5   *History of the Army Ordnance Services*, Forbes, Vol.2, Medici, 1928, p.107.
6   *Arms and the Wizard*, R.J.Q. Adams, Texas A&M Press, 1978, p.13.
7   *Arms and the Wizard*, R.J.Q. Adams, Texas A&M Press, 1978, p.10.
8   *The Great Munition Feat 1914–1918*, George A.B. Dewar, Constable and Company, 1921, p.60.
9   *The Great Munition Feat 1914–1918*, George A.B. Dewar, Constable and Company, 1921, p.63.
10 *Vickers: A History*, Scott, J.D., Weidenfeld & Nicolson, 1962, p.97.
11 *Vickers: A History*, Scott, J.D., Weidenfeld & Nicolson, 1962, p.40.
12 *William Armstrong, Magician of the North*, Henrietta Heald, Kindle edition.
13 *Vickers: A History*, Scott, J.D., Weidenfeld & Nicolson, 1962, p.28.
14 *William Armstrong, Magician of the North*, Henrietta Heald, Kindle, loc. 2088.
15 The Coventry Ordnance Works Limited, Coventry History Centre.
16 The Coventry Ordnance Works Limited, Coventry History Centre.
17 *Beardmore: The History of a Scottish Industrial Giant*, J.R. Hume, Heinemann, 1979, p.105.
18 *Daimler*, Alan Townsin, Ian Allan, 2000, p.16.
19 *The Other Battle: Being a history of the Birmingham Small Arms Co. Ltd., with special reference to the war achievements of B.S.A. Guns Ltd., B.S.A. Cycles Ltd,* Donovan M. Ward, Birmingham Small Arms Co. Limited, Ben Johnson & Co., 1946.
20 *The Other Battle*, 1946, p.25.

21 *Arms and the Wizard*, R.J.Q. Adams, Texas A&M Press, 1978, p.7.
22 *The Great Munition Feat 1914–1918*, George A.B. Dewar, Constable and Company, 1921, p.103.
23 *Vickers: A History*, Scott, J.D., Weidenfeld & Nicolson, 1962.
24 *The Other Battle*, 1946, p.28.
25 *The Great Munition Feat 1914–1918*, George A.B. Dewar, Constable and Company, 1921, p.7.
26 Vickers: A History, Scott, J.D., Weidenfeld & Nicolson, 1962, p.99.
27 Vickers: A History, Scott, J.D., Weidenfeld & Nicolson, 1962, p.107.
28 *The Wartime Production of Sir W.G. Armstrong*, Whitworth & Co., Ltd, 1919, p.8.
29 *Beardmore: The History of a Scottish Industrial Giant*, J.R. Hume, Heinemann, 1979, p.106.
30 *Getting to the Root of the Matter: The Mobilisation of the British Army Logistics for the First World War*, Major W.E. Campbell, thesis at RLC Archive.
31 Kitchener, Magnus, 331 quote in *Arms and the Wizard*, p.16.
32 *Vickers: A History*, Scott, J.D., Weidenfeld & Nicolson, 1962, p.100.
33 National Archives, MUN 6/7/170/28).
34 *Arms and the Wizard*, R.J.Q. Adams, Texas A&M Press, 1978, p.18.
35 *Britain America and the Sinews of War 1914–1918*, Kathleen Burk, George Allen & Unwin, 1985, p.15.
36 National Archives, MUN 5/6/170/23.
37 *The Great Munition Feat 1914–1918*, George A.B. Dewar, Constable and Company, 1921, p.17.
38 von Dunlop private papers, IWM.
39 von Dunlop private papers, IWM.
40 *Vickers: A History*, Scott, J.D., Weidenfeld & Nicolson, 1962, p.101.
41 *Beardmore: The History of a Scottish Industrial Giant*, J.R. Hume, Heinemann, 1979, p.117.
42 *The Great Munition Feat 1914–1918*, George A.B. Dewar, Constable and Company, 1921, p.32.
43 *History of the Army Ordnance Services*, Forbes, Vol.3, Medici, 1928, p.196.
44 Lecture on the Army Ordnance Department, its organisation and duties at home and in the field delivered to Officers of Staff Courses, Clare College, Cambridge by Lieutenant Colonel T.B.A. Leahy, 30 September 1916, RLC Archive.
45 Synopsis of Lectures by F.K. Puckle, Ch. II p.5, RLC Archive.
46 *The Royal Army Service Corps: A History of Transport and Supply in the British Army*, R.H. Beadon, Cambridge University Press, 1931.
47 *A Short History of the Army Ordnance Department Royal Arsenal & Dockyard, Woolwich*, AOD Memorial Fund, RLC archive, p.11.
48 *A Short History of the Army Ordnance Department Royal Arsenal & Dockyard, Woolwich*, AOD Memorial Fund, RLC archive, p.12.
49 *History of the Army Ordnance Services*, Forbes, Vol.3, Medici, 1928, p.193.
50 *London in the Nineteenth Century*, Jerry White, Vintage, London 2007, p.174.
51 *The Great Munition Feat 1914–1918*, George A.B. Dewar, Constable and Company, 1921, p.55.
52 Bill Williams archive.
53 *From Farms to Arms: A short history of the military in Didcot*, Alan Barker, RLC, p.2.
54 *From Farms to Arms: A short history of the military in Didcot*, Alan Barker, RLC, p.4.

Chapter 3

1 Hawkes Diary, RLC Archive.
2 *First World War*, Martin Gilbert, Harper Collins, 1995, p.125.
3 *History of the Army Ordnance Services*, Forbes, Vol.3, Medici, 1928, p.212.
4 *RAOC Gazette*, September 1934.
5 *History of the Army Ordnance Services*, Forbes, Vol.3, Medici, 1928, p.222.
6 *History of the Army Ordnance Services*, Forbes, Vol.3, Medici, 1928, p.224.
7 *History of the Army Ordnance Services*, Forbes, Vol.3, Medici, 1928, p.227.
8 *History of the Army Ordnance Services*, Forbes, Vol.3, Medici, 1928, p.232.
9 Hawkes Diary, RLC Archive.
10 *First World War*, Martin Gilbert, Harper Collins, 1995, p.191.
11 *History of the Army Ordnance Services*, Forbes, Vol.3, Medici, 1928, p.237.
12 *War on Wheels*, Philip Hamlyn Williams, The History Press, 2016. p.129.
13 Routh's letters, RLC Archive.
14 *History of the Army Ordnance Services*, Forbes, Vol.3, Medici, 1928, p.298.
15 'Chasing Von Lettow-Vorbeck', Richard Pullen.

Chapter 4

1 *Arms and the Wizard*, R.J.Q. Adams, Texas A&M Press, 1978.
2 *Arms and the Wizard*, R.J.Q. Adams, Texas A&M Press, 1978, pp.53–54.
3 *Arms and the Wizard*, R.J.Q. Adams, Texas A&M Press, 1978, p.42.
4 *Arms and the Wizard*, R.J.Q. Adams, Texas A&M Press, 1978, p.43.
5 *The Great Munition Feat 1914–1918*, George A.B. Dewar, Constable and Company, 1921, p.44.
6 *A Man of Push and Go: The Life of George Macaulay Booth*, Duncan Crow, Rupert Hart-Davis, 1965, p.90.
7 *The Great Munition Feat 1914–1918*, George A.B. Dewar, Constable and Company, 1921, p.113.
8 *A Man of Push and Go: The Life of George Macaulay Booth*, Duncan Crow, Rupert Hart-Davis, London 1965, p.111.
9 Chilwell story: V C factory and ordnance depot, M.J. Haslam, *RAOC Gazette*, 1982 RLC Archive.
10 Chilwell story: V C factory and ordnance depot, M.J. Haslam, *RAOC Gazette*, 1982, 13 RLC Archive.
11 *A Short History of the National Shell Filling Factory Chilwell, Notts.*
12 Chilwell story: V C factory and ordnance depot, M.J. Haslam, *RAOC Gazette*, 1982, RLC Archive.
13 Perks family archive.
14 Chilwell story: V C factory and ordnance depot., M.J. Haslam, *RAOC Gazette*, 1982, RLC Archive.
15 National Archives, WO 95/60/4 Lecture given on ammunition supply.
16 *Coventry and the Great War*, David McGrory, Amberley, 2016, pp.19–20.
17 *Midland Daily Telegraph*, 30 June 1922.
18 *We Re-invented the Wheel*, Ron Vice, Dunlop Aerospace Limited 2003, p.21.
19 *Arms and the Wizard*, R.J.Q. Adams, Texas A&M Press, 1978, p.100.

20 *Arms and the Wizard*, R.J.Q. Adams, Texas A&M Press, 1978, p.114.
21 *Arms and the Wizard*, R.J.Q. Adams, Texas A&M Press, 1978, p.116.
22 *Arms and the Wizard*, R.J.Q. Adams, Texas A&M Press, 1978, p.116.
23 National Archives, MUN 5/348/342/1.
24 National Archives, MUN 5/348/324/1.
25 National Archives, MUN 4/3622 Ministry of Munitions Journal 205.
26 *Labour Supply and Regulation*, Wolfe, pp.169–170.
27 *Arms and the Wizard*, R.J.Q. Adams, Texas A&M Press, 1978, p.136, Lloyd George War Memoirs Vol.II p.75.
28 von Dunlop private papers, IWM.
29 von Dunlop private papers, IWM.
30 *Arms and the Wizard*, R.J.Q. Adams, Texas A&M Press, 1978, p.140, Lloyd George War Memoirs Vol.II p.88–89.
31 *Arms and the Wizard*, R.J.Q. Adams, Texas A&M Press, 1978, p.138.
32 National Archives, MUN 5/10/200/2.
33 National Archives.
34 National Archives, MUN 5/119/700/6/9.
35 The Ministry of Munitions Journal, No. 6, May 1917, pp.165–7, National Archives.
36 National Archives, MUN 5/384/1610/4.
37 National Archives, MUN 5/384/1610/14.
38 National Archives, MUN 5/384/1610/7.
39 National Archives, MUN 5/384/1610/17.
40 Ordnance, Ch.3 p.8.
41 National Archives, MUN 5/195/1600/15.
42 *The Great Munition Feat 1914–1918*, George A.B. Dewar, Constable and Company, 1921, p.216.
43 *The Great Munition Feat 1914–1918*, George A.B. Dewar, Constable and Company, 1921, p.224.
44 National Archives, MUN 4/3622, Ministry of Munitions Journal, p.107.

Chapter 5

1   *A DADOS in France*, Lieutenant Colonel Omond RAOC, RLC Archive, p. 11.
2   Lecture on the Army Ordnance Department, its organisation and duties at home and in the field delivered to Officers of Staff Courses, Clare College, Cambridge by Lieutenant Colonel T.B.A. Leahy, 30 September 1916, RLC Archive.
3   Brigadier Leahy papers, RLC Archive.
4   LHW papers and War Diaries in the National Archives.
5   *History of the Army Ordnance Services*, Forbes, Vol. 3, Medici, 1928, p.40.
6   *History of the Army Ordnance Services*, Forbes, Vol. 3, Medici, 1928, p.82.
7   Issue 1, 22 January 1916, *AOC Workshops Gazette*, Editor was Lance Corporal J.G. Purcell, Censor Lieutenant Groundwater and Publisher Private Wookey, RLC Archive.
8   *AOC Workshops Gazette*, RLC Archive.
9   Lecture on the Army Ordnance Department, its organisation and duties at home and in the field delivered to Officers of Staff Courses, Clare College, Cambridge by Lieutenant Colonel T.B.A. Leahy, 30 September 1916, RLC Archive.
10 *History of the Army Ordnance Services*, Forbes, Vol.3, Medici, 1928, p.99.

11   Lecture on the Army Ordnance Department, its organisation and duties at home and in the field delivered to Officers of Staff Courses, Clare College, Cambridge by Lieutenant Colonel T.B.A. Leahy, 30 September 1916, RLC Archive.

12   *History of the Army Ordnance Services*, Forbes, Vol.3, Medici, 1928, p.106.

13   *History of the Army Ordnance Services*, Forbes, Vol.3, Medici, 1928, p.124.

14   IWM War Diaries of 8OD.

15   *History of the Army Ordnance Services*, Forbes, Vol.3, Medici, 1928, p.90.

16   *The History of the 19th Division 1914–1918*, Everard Wyrall, Edward Arnold, 1932, p.22.

17   *The History of the 19th Division 1914–1918*, Everard Wyrall, Edward Arnold, 1932, p.38.

18   Bill Williams archive.

19   *Ordnance*, Chapter 8.

20   Bill Williams archive.

21   *The History of the 19th Division 1914–1918*, Everard Wyrall, Edward Arnold, 1932, p.114.

22   *RAOC Gazette*, RLC Archive.

Chapter 6

1   *The Landships of* Richard Pullen, Tucann Books, 2007, p.15.

2   *The Great Munition Feat 1914–1918*, George A.B. Dewar, Constable and Company, 1921, p.227.

3   *A DADOS in France*, Lieutenant J.S. Omond, RLC Archive, p.55.

4   *Dunlop Story*, James McMillan, Weidenfeld and Nicholson, 1989.

5   *Wolseley: A Saga of the Motor Industry*, St John C. Nixon, G.T. Foulis, 1949, p.106.

6   *Wolseley: A Saga of the Motor Industry*, St John C. Nixon, G.T. Foulis, 1949, p.98.

7   *Sure as the Sunrise: A History of Albion Motors*, Sam McKinstry, John Donald, 1997, p.42.

8   *The First Fifty Years Leyland Motors Limited* (reprinted from a series of articles published in 'The Leyland Journal' in May, July, September and November) 1946, p.29.

9   *Sure as the Sunrise: A History of Albion Motors*, Sam McKinstry, John Donald, 1997, p.33.

10   *The First Fifty Years Leyland Motors Limited* p.35.

11   *Sure as the Sunrise: A History of Albion Motors*, Sam McKinstry, John Donald, 1997, p.19.

12   *Sure as the Sunrise: A History of Albion Motors*, Sam McKinstry, John Donald, 1997, p.56.

13   *Glory Days Foden*, B.S. Wilson, Ian Allan, 2000, p.10.

14   *Daimler*, Alan Townsin, Ian Allan, 2000, p.21.

15   *Daimler*, Alan Townsin, Ian Allan, 2000, p.23.

16   *AEC*, Alan Townsin, Ian Allan, Shepperton, 1998, p.7.

17   *AEC*, Alan Townsin, Ian Allan, Shepperton, 1998, p.13.

18   *AEC*, Alan Townsin, Ian Allan, Shepperton, 1998, p.17.

19   *Thornycroft*, Alan Townsin, Ian Allan, 2001, p.24.

20   *Humber Story 1868-1932*, A.B. Demaus and J.C. Tarring, Alan Sutton, 1989, p.55.

21   *The Complete Bentley*, Eric Dymock, Dove Publishing, 2008, p.13.

22   *Humber Story 1868–1932*, A.B. Demaus and J.C. Tarring, Alan Sutton, 1989, p.84.

23   *Rootes Commercial Vehicles*, L. Geary, Ian Henry, Romford, 1993.

24   *Rootes Commercial Vehicles*, L. Geary, Ian Henry, Romford, 1993, p.89.

25   *AJS, Star and Sunbeam*, The PSV Circle, 2001, p.64.

26   *Herbert Austin – The British Motor Car Industry to 1941*, Roy Church, Europa, 1979, p.13.

27   *Wolseley: A Saga of the Motor Industry*, St John C. Nixon, G.T. Foulis, 1949, p.94.

28   *The Diary of an Old Contemptible*, Kindle edition, loc. 4644.

29 *Herbert Austin – The British Motor Car Industry to 1941*, Roy Church, Europa, 1979, p.43.
30 *The Life of Lord Nuffield*, Andrews and Brunner, Blackwell, 1955, p.80.
31 *War on Wheels.*
32 *The Best Twin: The Story of the Douglas Motor Cycle*, J.R. Clew, Goose and Son, 1974, p.51.
33 *The Best Twin: The Story of the Douglas Motor Cycle*, J.R. Clew, Goose and Son, 1974, p.50.
34 *The Best Twin: The Story of the Douglas Motor Cycle*, J.R. Clew, Goose and Son, 1974, p.54.
35 *The Story of Triumph Motor Cycles*, Harry Louis and Bob Currie, Patrick Stephens Ltd, 1975, 1983, p.12.
36 *The Story of Triumph Motor Cycles*, Harry Louis and Bob Currie, Patrick Stephens Ltd, 1975, 1983, p.13.
37 *The World Encyclopaedia of Tanks*, George Forty, Loenz Books, 2014, p.16.
38 *The World Encyclopaedia of Armoured Fighting Vehicles*, Jack Livesey, Lorenz Books, 2014, p.14.
39 *Rolls-Royce*, George Oliver, Haynes Publishing, 1988, p.64.
40 *First World War*, Martin Gilbert, Harper Collins, 1995, p.199.
41 *First World War*, Martin Gilbert, Harper Collins, 1995, p.124.
42 *The Dunlop Story*, p.42.
43 Private papers of L.S. Jeffcoate, RLC Archive.
44 *The Landships of Lincoln*, Richard Pullen, Tucann Books, 2007, p.10.
45 *Vickers: A History*, Scott, J.D., Weidenfeld & Nicolson, 1962, p.107.
46 *The Landships of Lincoln*, Richard Pullen, Tucann Books, 2007, p.15.
47 *One Hundred Years of Good Company: The Story of Ruston & Hornsby*, Bernard Newman, 1957, p.62.
48 *The Landships of Lincoln*, Richard Pullen, Tucann Books, 2007.
49 *The Dunlop Story*, p.44.
50 *War on Wheels.*
51 *The Dunlop Story*, p.42.
52 *Cambrai: The First Tank Battle 1917*, A.J. Smithers, Leo Cooper, 1992, p.48.
53 *The Landships of* Richard Pullen, Tucann Books, 2007, p.48.
54 *First World War*, Martin Gilbert, Harper Collins, 1995, p.286.
55 *Metro-Cammell: 150 Years of Craftsmanship*, Keith Beddoes, Colin and Stephen Wheeler, Runpast Publishing, 1999, p.23.
56 *The Landships of* Richard Pullen, Tucann Books, Lincoln 2007, p.54.
57 *Cambrai: The First Tank Battle 1917*, A.J. Smithers, Leo Cooper, 1992, p.49.
58 National Archives, WO 95 60 4, War History of the RAOC with Heavy Branch MGC and Tank Corps.
59 *Cambrai: The First Tank Battle 1917*, A.J. Smithers, Leo Cooper, 1992, p.83.
60 *Cambrai: The First Tank Battle 1917*, A.J. Smithers, Leo Cooper, 1992, p.83.
61 *Cambrai: The First Tank Battle 1917*, A.J. Smithers, Leo Cooper, 1992, p.102.
62 *First World War*, Martin Gilbert, Harper Collins, 1995, p.379.
63 Greenhalgh, Elizabeth. 'Technology Development in Coalition: The Case of the First World War Tank.' *The International History Review*, vol. 22, no. 4, 2000, pp.806–836. *JSTOR*, www.jstor.org/stable/40108526.
64 *The Great Munition Feat 1914–1918*, George A.B. Dewar, Constable and Company, 1921, 182
65 *The Landships of* Richard Pullen, Tucann Books, 2007, p.90.

Chapter 7

1   *History of the Army Ordnance Services*, Forbes, Vol.3, Medici, 1928, p.212.
2   *The Landships of Lincoln,* Richard Pullen, Tucann Books, 2007, p.54.
3   *RAOC Gazette*, September 1934.
4   *Railways of the Great War*, Colette Hooper, Bantam Press, 2014.
5   *History of the Army Ordnance Services*, Forbes, Vol.3, Medici, 1928, p.260.
6   *History of the Army Ordnance Services*, Forbes, Vol.3, Medici, 1928, p.263.
7   IWM Private papers of Thomas Cook.
8   RLC Archive report by Brigadier Perry.
9   *War on Wheels*.
10 Report by Brigadier Perry, RLC Archive.
11 Report by Howell Jones, RLC Archive.
12 *Diary of an Old Contemptible*, Kindle edition, loc. 4563.
13 *History of the Army Ordnance Services*, Forbes, Vol. 3, Medici, 1928, p.308.
14 Bill Williams archive.
15 *History of the Army Ordnance Services*, Forbes, Vol. 3, Medici, 1928, p.317.

Chapter 8

1   *History of the Studebaker Corporation*, Albert Russel Erskine, 1924, p.54.
2   *A DADOS in France*, Lieutenant Colonel Omond RAOC, RLC Archive, p.13.
3   *Benjamin Holt & Caterpillar Tracks & Combines*, Reynold M. Wik, American Society of Agricultural Engineers, 1984, p.48.
4   *Benjamin Holt & Caterpillar Tracks & Combines*, Reynold M. Wik, American Society of Agricultural Engineers, 1984, p.82.
5   *Benjamin Holt & Caterpillar Tracks & Combines*, Reynold M. Wik, American Society of Agricultural Engineers, 1984, p.83; Major-General John J. Pershing, 'Motor Truck Transportation in Mexico,' *Texas Motorist*, April 1917, pp.5–7.
6   *Benjamin Holt & Caterpillar Tracks & Combines*, Reynold M. Wik, American Society of Agricultural Engineers, 1984, p.84; DeHann, 'Holt Tractor', p.14. Interview with William K. Holt, 8 November 1977.
7   *Britain, America and the Sinews of War 1914–1918*, Kathleen Burk, George Allen and Unwin, 1985, p.44.
8   *Britain, America and the Sinews of War 1914–1918*, Kathleen Burk, George Allen and Unwin, 1985, p.22.
9   *Britain, America and the Sinews of War 1914–1918*, Kathleen Burk, George Allen and Unwin, 1985, p.33.
10 *Britain, America and the Sinews of War 1914–1918*, Kathleen Burk, George Allen and Unwin, 1985, p.24.
11 *Britain, America and the Sinews of War 1914–1918*, Kathleen Burk, George Allen and Unwin, 1985, p.41.
12 *Britain, America and the Sinews of War 1914–1918*, Kathleen Burk, George Allen and Unwin, 1985, p.223.
13 *Britain, America and the Sinews of War 1914–1918*, Kathleen Burk, George Allen and Unwin, 1985, p.74.
14 *First World War*, Martin Gilbert, Harper Collins, 1995, p.342.

15 *First World War*, Martin Gilbert, Harper Collins, 1995, p.359.

16 *First World War*, Martin Gilbert, Harper Collins, 1995, p.419.

17 *The Neck of the Bottle, George W. Goethals and the Reorganisation of the US Army Supply System, 1917–1918*, Phyllis A. Zimmerman, Texas A&M University Press, 1992, p.21.

18 *The Neck of the Bottle, George W. Goethals and the Reorganisation of the US Army Supply System, 1917–1918*, Phyllis A. Zimmerman, Texas A&M University Press, 1992, p.24.

19 *The Army behind the Army*, E. Alexander Powell, Charles Scribner's Sons, 1919, p.147.

20 *Ford in the Service of America*, Timothy J. O'Callaghan, p.6.

21 *Ford in the Service of America*, Timothy J. O'Callaghan, p.8.

22 *Ford in the Service of America*, Timothy J. O'Callaghan, p.9.

23 *Ford in the Service of America*, Timothy J. O'Callaghan, p.9.

24 *Ford in the Service of America*, Timothy J. O'Callaghan, p.24.

25 *General Motors: The first 75 years of transportation products*, General Motors, p.34.

26 *General Motors: The first 75 years of transportation products*, General Motors, p.34.

27 *The Army behind the Army*, E. Alexander Powell, Charles Scribner's Sons, 1919, p.241.

28 *The Army behind the Army*, E. Alexander Powell, Charles Scribner's Sons, 1919, p.226.

29 *Britain, America and the Sinews of War 1914–1918*, Kathleen Burk, George Allen and Unwin, 1985, p.124.

30 *Britain, America and the Sinews of War 1914–1918*, Kathleen Burk, George Allen and Unwin, 1985, p.129.

31 *Britain, America and the Sinews of War 1914–1918*, Kathleen Burk, George Allen and Unwin, 1985, p.170.

32 Leahy private papers, RLC Archive.

33 'Great Britain for Democracy', a speech given by Lt Col G.G. Woodward, 25 September 1918, RLC Archive.

34 *Britain, America and the Sinews of War 1914–1918*, Kathleen Burk, George Allen and Unwin, 1985, p.191.

Chapter 9

1 Captain Omond papers, RLC Archive.

2 Captain Omond papers, RLC Archive.

3 Captain Hawkes' papers, RLC Archive.

4 *History of the Army Ordnance Services*, Forbes, Vol.3, Medici, 1928, p.156.

5 Report by Captain Alaway, RLC Archive.

6 *The History of the 19th Division 1914–1918*, Everard Wyrall, Edward Arnold, p.172.

7 *War on Wheels*, Philip Hamlyn Williams, The History Press, 2016, p.39.

8 Private Papers of Lieutenant Colonel W.E. Fairholme, IWM.

9 War Diaries 8OD, IWM.

10 *First World War*, Martin Gilbert, Harper Collins 1995, p.457.

11 *History of the Army Ordnance Services*, Forbes, Vol.3, Medici, 1928, p.181.

12 *History of the Army Ordnance Services*, Forbes, Vol.3, Medici, 1928, p.180.

13 Captain Omond papers, RLC Archive.

BIBLIOGRAPHY

A Man of Push and Go: The Life of George Macaulay Booth, Duncan Crow (London: Rupert Hart-Davis, 1965)

A Short History of the Army Ordnance Department Royal Arsenal & Dockyard, Woolwich, AOD Memorial Fund, RLC Archive

AEC, Alan Townsin (Shepperton: Ian Allan, 1998)

A.J.S., Star and Sunbeam (Harrow: The PSV Circle, 2001)

Arms and the Wizard, R.J.Q. Adams (Texas A&M Press, 1978)

Beardmore: The History of a Scottish Industrial Giant, J.R. Hume and Michael S. Moss (London: Heinemann, 1979)

Benjamin Holt & Caterpillars: Tracks & Combines, Reynold M. Wik (St Joseph, MI: American Society of Agricultural Engineers, 1984)

Britain, America and the Sinews of War, 1914–1918, Kathleen Burk (London: George Allen & Unwin, 1985)

Cambrai: The First Tank Battle 1917, A.J. Smithers (London: Leo Cooper, 1992)

Daimler, Alan Townsin (Shepperton: Ian Allan, 2000)

The Dunlop Story, James McMillan (London: Weidenfeld and Nicolson, 1989)

First World War, Martin Gilbert (London: Harper Collins, 1995)

Foden, B.S. Wilson (Shepperton: Ian Allan, 2000)

Ford in the Service of America, Timothy J. O'Callaghan (Jefferson, N.C: MacFarland & Co., 2009)

General Motors: The First 75 Years of Transportation Products, General Motors (Princeton, NJ: Automobile Quarterly Publications, 1983)

Herbert Austin: The British Motor Car Industry to 1941, Roy Church (London: Europa, 1979)

History of the Army Ordnance Services Vol. 3, A. Forbes (London, Medici Society, 1929)

History of the Studebaker Corporation, Albert Russel Erskine (South Bend Ind: Studebaker Corp, 1924)

London in the 19th Century, Jerry White (London: Vintage, 2007)

Metro-Cammell: 150 Years of Craftsmanship, Keith Beddoes, Colin and Stephen Wheeler (Cheltenham: Runpast Publishing, 1999)

One Hundred Years of Good Company: The Story of Ruston & Hornsby, Bernard Newman (Lincoln: Ruston & Hornsby, 1957)

Railways of the Great War, Colette Hooper (London: Bantam Press, 2014)

Rolls-Royce: The Best Car in the World, George Oliver (Sparkford: Haynes Publishing, 1988)

Rootes Commercial Vehicles, L. Geary (Romford: Ian Henry, 1993)

Sure as the Sunrise: A History of Albion Motors, Sam McKinstry (Edinburgh: John Donald, 1997)

The Army behind the Army, E. Alexander Powell (New York: Charles Scribner's Sons, 1919)

The Best Twin: The Story of the Douglas Motor Cycle, J.R. Clew (Norwich: Goose and Son, 1974)

The Chilwell Story: VC Factory and Ordnance Depot, M.J. Haslam (England: RAOC Gazette, 1982)

The Complete Bentley, Eric Dymock (Rothesay: Dove Publishing, 2008)

The Coventry Ordnance Works Limited, Coventry History Centre

The Diary of an Old Contemptible, Peter Downham, Kindle edition (Barnsley: Pen & Sword, 2005)

The First Fifty Years, Leyland Motors Limited, Leyland Motors (Lancashire: Leyland Motors Ltd, 1949)

The Great Munition Feat, 1914–1918, George A.B. Dewar (London: Constable and Company, 1921)

The History of the 19th Division 1914–1918, Everard Wyrall (London: Edward Arnold, 1932)

The Humber Story 1868–1932, A.B. Demaus and J.C. Tarring (Stroud: Alan Sutton, 1989)

The Landships of Lincoln, Richard Pullen, 2nd ed. (Lincoln: Tucann Books, 2007)

The Life of Lord Nuffield, P.W.S. Andrews and Elizabeth Brunner (Oxford: Basil Blackwell, 1955)

The Neck of the Bottle: George W. Goethals and the Reorganisation of the US Army Supply System, 1917–1918, Phyllis A. Zimmerman (Texas: Texas A&M University Press, 1992)

The Other Battle: Being a History of the Birmingham Small Arms Co. Ltd., with special reference to the war achievements of B.S.A. Guns Ltd., B.S.A. Cycles Ltd, and the Other Subsidiary Companies Directly Administered from the Head Office of the Parent Company at Small Heath, Birmingham, Donovan M. Ward (York: Ben Johnson & Co. 1946)

The Royal Army Service Corps: A History of Transport and Supply in the British Army, R.H. Beadon (Cambridge University Press, 1931)

The Royal Arsenal Woolwich, Wesley Harry (London: MOD, 1987)

The Story of Triumph Motor Cycles, Harry Louis and Bob Currie, 4th ed. (Cambridge: Patrick Stephens Ltd, 1983)

The War Work of Sir W.G. Armstrong (Whitworth & Co., Ltd, 1919)

The Wheelwright's Shop, George Sturt, Kindle edition, reprint (Home Farm Books, 2013)

The World Encyclopedia of Armoured Fighting Vehicles, Jack Livesey (London: Lorenz Books, 2014)

The World Encyclopedia of Tanks, George Forty (London: Lorenz Books, 2014)

Thornycroft, Alan Townsin (Shepperton: Ian Allan, 2001)

To the Warrior His Arms: The Story of the Royal Army Ordnance Corps, Frank Steer (Barnsley: Pen & Sword, 2005)

Vickers: A History, J.D. Scott (London: Weidenfeld & Nicolson, 1962)

War on Wheels, Philip Hamlyn Williams (Stroud: The History Press, 2016)

We Re-invented the Wheel, Ron Vice (Coventry: Dunlop Aerospace Limited, 2003)

William Armstrong: Magician of the North, Henrietta Heald, Kindle edition (Newcastle Upon Tyne: Northumbria University Press, 2010)

Wolseley: A Saga of the Motor Industry, St John C. Nixon (London: G.T. Foulis, 1949)